CURIOSITIES OF THE CHURCH; STUDIES OF CURIOUS CUSTOMS, SEVICES RECORDS

CURIOSITIES OF THE CHURCH; STUDIES OF CURIOUS CUSTOMS, SEVICES RECORDS

William Andrews

www.General-Books.net

Publication Data:

Title: Curiosities of the Church
Subtitle: Studies of Curious Customs, Sevices Records
Author: William Andrews
Reprinted: 2010, General Books, Memphis, Tennessee, USA
Publisher: Methuen
Publication date: 1895
Subjects: Christian antiquities
Great Britain
Architecture / Religious Buildings
Art / Subjects Themes / Religious
Religion / Christianity / Anglican
Religion / Christianity / History
Religion / Christianity / Protestant
Religion / Antiquities Archaeology
Religion / Christian Church / History
BISAC subject codes: ART035000, REL003000, REL015000, REL053000, REL072000, REL108020

How We Made This Book for You
We made this book exclusively for you using patented Print on Demand technology.
First we scanned the original rare book using a robot which automatically flipped and photographed each page.
We automated the typing, proof reading and design of this book using Optical Character Recognition (OCR) software on the scanned copy. That let us keep your cost as low as possible.
If a book is very old, worn and the type is faded, this can result in numerous typos or missing text. This is also why our books don't have illustrations; the OCR software can't distinguish between an illustration and a smudge.
We understand how annoying typos, missing text or illustrations, foot notes in the text or an index that doesn't work, can be. That's why we provide a free digital copy of most books exactly as they were originally published. You can also use this PDF edition to read the book on the go. Simply go to our website (www.general-books.net) to check availability. And we provide a free trial membership in our book club so you can get free copies of other editions or related books.
OCR is not a perfect solution but we feel it's more important to make books available for a low price than not at all. So we warn readers on our website and in the descriptions we provide to book sellers that our books don't have illustrations and may have numerous typos or missing text. We also provide excerpts from books to book sellers and on our website so you can preview the quality of the book before buying it.
If you would prefer that we manually type, proof read and design your book so that it's perfect, simply contact us for the cost. Since many of our books only sell one or two copies, we have to split the production costs between those one or two buyers.

Frequently Asked Questions

Why are there so many typos in my paperback?
We created your book using OCR software that includes an automated spell check. Our OCR software is 99 percent accurate if the book is in good condition. Therefore, we try to get several copies of a book to get the best possible accuracy (which is very difficult for rare books more than a hundred years old). However, with up to 3,500 characters per page, even one percent is an annoying number of typos. We would really like to manually proof read and correct the typos. But since many of our books only sell a couple of copies that could add hundreds of dollars to the cover price. And nobody wants to pay that. If you need to see the original text, please check our website for a downloadable copy.

Why is the index and table of contents missing (or not working) from my paperback?
After we re-typeset and designed your book, the page numbers change so the old index and table of contents no longer work. Therefore, we usually remove them. We dislike publishing books without indexes and contents as much as you dislike buying them. But many of our books only sell a couple of copies. So manually creating a new index and table of contents could add more than a hundred dollars to the cover price. And nobody wants to pay that. If you need to see the original index, please check our website for a downloadable copy.

Why are illustrations missing from my paperback?
We created your book using OCR software. Our OCR software can't distinguish between an illustration and a smudge or library stamp so it ignores everything except type. We would really like to manually scan and add the illustrations. But many of our books only sell a couple of copies so that could add more than a hundred dollars to the cover price. And nobody wants to pay that. If you need to see the original illustrations, please check our website for a downloadable copy.

Why is text missing from my paperback?
We created your book using a robot who turned and photographed each page. Our robot is 99 percent accurate. But sometimes two pages stick together. And sometimes a page may even be missing from our copy of the book. We would really like to manually scan each page. But many of our books only sell a couple of copies so that could add more than a hundred dollars to the cover price. And nobody wants to pay that. If you would like to check the original book for the missing text, please check our website for a downloadable copy.

CURIOSITIES OF THE CHURCH; STUDIES OF CURIOUS CUSTOMS, SEVICES RECORDS

CURIOUS CHURCH CUSTOMS.

Sports in Cburcbes.

By Rev. J. Charles Cox, Ll. d., F. s. a.

IN mediaeval and feudal days, as is well-known, our parish churches, in addition to their primary purpose of providing places for public worship and religious instruction, commonly served for various secular objects. They were used for manorial courts and other legal purposes of an entirely civil character, as well as for the meeting of spiritual and ecclesiastical tribunals; they served, particularly in troublous times, for the storage of wool and for the safe-custody of treasure chests; and they occasionally gave shelter, as at fair times and during the parish wakes, to hucksters stalls, and to booths for the sale of victuals. Public opinion of those days saw nothing specially reprehensible in such uses of the churches, provided they were confined to the naves, and did not interfere with divine service, more particularly on the Sunday and festivals.

This being the case, it is not surprising to find that churches were, from time to time, used for what may fairly be termed "sports," or amusements.

The custom, once so prevalent in the great churches, of appointing a Boy-Bishop, or Nicholas-Bishop, which is so abhorrent to modern ideas of reverence, and which gradually developed in extravagance, had a praiseworthy commencement. It originated in the idea of rewarding, after a religious fashion, the most deserving choir-boy or scholar of the church-school. The selected lad was appointed bishop of the boys on St. Nicholas Day (the patron saint of boys) during the solemn singing of the Magnificat, and was vested in special pontificals of a small size. He held the office from December 6th (St. Nicholas Day) to December 28th (Holy Innocents). " The custom," says Precentor Walcott, "prevailed in the great schools of Winchester and Eton, and was perpetuated by Dean Colet in his foundation of St. Pauls, no doubt as a stimulus to Christian ambition in the boy, just as the mitre and staff are painted as the reward of learning on the scrolls of Winchester, or in honour of the Holy Child Jesus."

The following is the statute of Dean Colet, A. d. 1518, on this subject:–"All these children shall, every Childermas Daye, come to Paules Churche, and hear the Childe Bishops sermone; and after be at the hyghe masse, and each of them offer a 1d. to the Childe Bishop, and with them maistors and surveyors of the scole."

The ceremonies attached to this boyish parody of a most solemn office varied considerably, but it is known to have existed in all the cathedral churches of France and Spain, as well as in many parts of Germany and Switzerland. In England, every cathedral, which possesses post-rsformation records, yields abundant evidence of the Child-Bishop customs. We found interesting mention of it in several places when setting in order the chaotic mass of capitular muniments at Lichfield. An inventory of 1345 names four small choir copes for the use of boys on the feast of Holy Innocents. The next century names a mitre, cope, sandals, gloves, and staff for the Nicholas Bishop. An invariable part of the proceedings seems to have been a sermon from the Boy Bishop, delivered from the usual pulpit. He was doubtless well drilled in the discourse by the chancellor, or by his substitute, the choir school master. Indeed, several of the sermons that were learnt by rote by the Boy Bishop are still extant. At Salisbury, the whole details are set forth in the printed procession of the cathedral church. In the order of the procession, on the eve of Innocents Day, the dean and canons residentiary walked first, and were followed by the chaplains; the boy-bishop, with his boy-prebendaries, closing the procession as the position of the greatest dignity. The boy-bishop and his attendants took the highest places in choir, the canons carrying the incense, tapers, etc. At the conclusion of compline the boy gave the benediction, and until the close of the procession on the following evening none of the clergy of any condition were allowed to ascend to the upper part of the sanctuary, which was reserved for the choir boys and their prelate.

In most churches the boys performed all the ceremonies, and said all the offices save mass during this period; in some they were even permitted to make a travesty of mass. On the Continent, a variety of indecent levities were by degrees admitted, such as the boy being dressed in a bishops robes reversed, and old shoes being burnt instead of incense; and when they had raised sufficient scandal in the church itself, they then paraded the streets, or sought to make levies in the market-place. To the credit of the church, it should be remarked that these excesses were on several occasions interdicted by pre-reformation councils, though apparently with but partial success. The Council of Basle, which sat in 1431, issued the following stringent canon:—" This sacred synod, detesting that foul abuse frequent in certain churches, in which, on certain festivals of the year, certain persons with a mitre, staff, and pontifical robes, bless men after the manner of bishops, others being clothed like kings and dukes, which is called the Feast of Fools, of Innocents, or of Children in certain countries; others practising vizarded and theatrical sports; others making trains and dances of men and women, move men to spectacles and cachin-nations; hath appointed and commanded as well ordinaries as deans and rectors of churches, under pain of suspension of all their ecclesiastical revenues for three months space, if they suffered these and such like plays and pastimes to be any more "exercised in the church, which ought to be the house of prayer, nor yet in the churchyard, and that they neglect not to punish the offender by ecclesiastical censures and other remedies of law."

Boy-bishoping was by no means confined in England to the cathedral and large collegiate churches, but it was so generally prevalent and popular that it appears to have prevailed where-ever there was a choir school, attached to to any church, whether in town or country. The churchwardens accounts of St. Mary Hill, London, 1485-6, contain the two following entries:–" Item, six copes for children of dyvers sortes. Item, a myter for a bishop at Seint Nycholas tyde, garnyshed with sylver and anelyd, and perles and counterfete stones." The same accounts make mention of the purchase of properties for a like purpose in 1549-50 during Queen Marys reign. We have met references to a like childrens pageant in comparatively out-of-the-way places of Yorkshire, Derbyshire, and West Somersetshire.

So far as England was concerned, the show of the boy-bishop, which the Church had failed to suppress or to keep within decent limits was summarily put an end to (save for a slight revival in the days of Mary Tudor) by a vigorous proclamation of Henry VIII. This proclamation, issued on July 22nd, 1542, thus concludes:–"Whereas heretofore dyvers and many superstitious and chyldish observancies have been used, and yet to this day are observed and kept in many and sundry partes of this realme, as upon Saint Nicholas, the Holie Innocents, and such like, the children be strangelie decked and apparayled to counterfeit priests, bishops and women, and to be ledde with songs and dances from house to house, blessing the people, and gathering of money; and boys do singe masse and preach in the pulpitt, with such unfutinge and inconvenient usages, rather to the derysyion than anie true glorie of God, or honour of His Sayntes. The Kynges Majestic wylleth and commandeth that henceforth all such superstitious observancies be left and duly extinguished throughout all this realm and dominions."

The writings of the early reformers, as well as allusions in secular literature of the sixteenth century, help to prove how well-known, nay almost universal, was this boyish sporting and strange burlesquing of things sacred throughout England In "The Catechism of the Offices of all Degrees," issued by Thomas Beacon, Chaplain to Archbishop Cranmer, in the time of Edward VI., occurs the following passage:–

"Father.–What if he preach aot, neither can preach?

Son.–Then is he a Nicholas bishop and an idol, and indeed no better than a painted bishop on a wall: yea, he is, as the prophet saith, A dumb dog, not able to bark; he is also, as our Saviour Christ saith Unsavoury salt, worth for nothing but to be cast out, and to be trodden under foot of men. Wo be to those rulers that set such idols and white daubed walls over the flock of Christ, whom he hath purchased with His precious blood! Horrible and great is their damnation."

At the first blush, any connection with dancing and church attendance or worship may seem profane and impossible; but further reflection at all events qualifies any too hasty generalisation. Emotions of joy and sorrow universally express themselves among mankind in movements and gestures of the body. Efforts were therefore made in early days, particularly among the more demonstrative people of the east and south, to reduce to measure, and to strengthen by unison, pleasureable emotions of joy. The dance is spoken of throughout the Old Testament as symbolical of rejoicing, and the rejoicing in their feasts is emphatically and repeatedly enjoined upon the Israelites. So, too, with both Romans and Egyptians, the dance, in certain circumstances, was associated with religibus ceremonies, and was intended to express the thankful worship of the body. The dances led by Miriam, by Jephthahs daughter, by Judith, and doubtless too by Deborah, soon occur to the mind. David also himself led the dance on the return of the Ark of God from its long exile; whilst from the mention in association of " damsels," "timbrels," and "dances" as elements of religious worship in Psalms cxvii, cxlix, and cl, it may be concluded that David incorporated these joyous movements in the formal rites of the established Tabernacle service. In later Judaism the dance certainly survived in the religious festivities of the feast of Tabernacles. It may therefore have come to pass that early Christians, realising the joyous feature of their special creed, expressing its constant, belief in the " resurrection of the body," may have desired in all honesty and innocency to occasionally associate the dance with festal service. The results were, however, unfortunate; pagan practices of a like character were, as a rule, of a licentious nature, and it became necessary to try and suppress all such forms of expression of joy or thanksgiving. St. Augustine mentions with abhorrence that dancers invaded the resting place of St. Cyprian at night and sang songs there, a custom that died out on the institution of vigils. Pope Eugenius II. (824-7) prohibited dancing in churches, thereby showing how usual the custom became. In 858 the Bishop of Orleans condemned the dancing of women in the presbytery on festivals. The Council of Avignon, which sat in 1209, prohibited the theatrical dances in churches which were sqmetimes the accompaniment of the vigils of Saints days. The Councils of Bourges in 1286, and of Bayeux in 130x3, condemned all dances which took place in church or churchyards. In the later mediaeval period Morris-dancing was associated with churches, and the wardens not infrequently had in their possession certain properties that were necessary for its due performance. The Morris-dancing was occasionally actually performed within the churches, that is in the nave or at the west end; the mummers not going forth on their Whitsuntide round until the first dance had been given within the sacred fabric. Nor is it difficult for the antiquary to trace the connection between the Morris-dancing and the active expression of Christianity. When the Fifth Crusade succeeded in effecting the capture of Constantinople, the Latins in their joy celebrated the event by solemn dances in the great church of St. Sophia. The usual, nay almost invariable, subject of the mumming-play, as apart from the miracle-play, was one drawn from the crusading legend, St. George rescuing a Christian maid from her Turkish masters was the usual stock piece, whilst the joy of victory was invariably celebrated in the Morris (that is the Moorish) dance.

The earliest of the Kingston-upon-Thames churchwarden accounts, which cover the last years of Henry VII. and the reign of Henry VIII., have various references to these dances, hi the inventory of church property for 1537-8 are enumerated:–. A fryer-s cote of russet and a kyrtele welted with red cloth, a mowrens (Moors) cote of buckram, and four morres daunsars cotes of white fustian spangelid, and too gryne satin cotes, and disarddes cote of cotton, and six payre of garters with belles."

In the recently published and highly-interesting churchwardens accounts of St. Marys, Reading, are the following entries for the year 1556-7:–

"Itm payed for the morrys daunsers and the mynstrelles mete and drinke at Whit-suntide iii. s. iiij. d

"Itm payed to them the Sondy after Mayday-xx. d

Pd to the painter for paynting of their Cottes-ii. s. viij. d

Pd for a peir of showes for the morris daunsers-iiij. s

Pd for iiij dozen belles for the morrys daunsers-ij. s

Pd for sowing of the morrys Cottes–.-vij. d

The churchwardens accounts of St. Helens, Abingdon, for the second year of Queen Elizabeth (1559) show that "two dozen of morres belles were bought by the parish for a shilling."

An injunction of Henry VIII. laid down the principle, now so generally accepted, that "all soberness, quietness, and godliness ought there (in the churches) to be used," and enjoined that " no Christian person should abuse the same by eating, drinking, buying, selling, playing, dancing, or with other profane or worldly matters." But this injunction was often treated as a dead letter up to the close of the century in which it was issued. In Stubbs " Anatomic of Abuses," first printed in 1585, we read:–

"The wild heades of the parish, flocking together, chuse them a grawnd captain of mischief, whom they innoble with the title of my Lord of Misrule. Then marche these heathen companie towards the church and churchyard, their pipers pypyng, drummers thonderyng, their stumpes dauncyng, their belles jynglyng, their handkerchefes swyngyng about their heads like madmen, their hobbie-horses and other monsters skyrmishyng amongst the throng; and in this sorte they go to the church (though the minister be at praier or preachyng) dauncing and swyngyng their handkerchiefs over their heads in the churche, like devilles incarnate, with such a confused noise that no man can heare his owne voyce. Then the foolish people, they looke, they stare, they laugh, they fleere, and mywnt upon the formes and pewes to see these goodly pageants solemnized in this sort. Then, after this, about the church they go againe and againe, and so fourthe into the churchyard, where they have commonly their summerhalls, their bowers, arbours and banquetyng houses set up, wherein they feast, banquet and dance all that day, and peradventure, all that night too, and thus these terrestrial furies spend the sabbath daie."

In the days of the antiquary, Sir John Aubrey, who died in 1697, there was Christmas dancing in. various Yorkshire churches, accompanied with songs of Yule.

The mounted reindeer antlers, as well as the dresses and other properties of the remarkable horn dancers of Abbots Bromley, Staffordshire, ate still kept in the parish church, where we recently had an opportunity of examining them when investigating the history of this highly interesting survival. The dance still continues year by year, and there seems no doubt that the tradition is true which assigned to the performers a preliminary dance through the churches before they started on their rounds through the parish and neighbourhood, collecting money for church purposes. There are those living who can recollect the accompanying music being played in the church porch, whilst the dancers executed their steps in the adjacent parts of the churchyard.

A singular and attractive relic of the custom of dancing in churches is still practiced three times a year in the great cathedral of Seville, namely on the feasts of the Immaculate Conception, and of Corpus Christi, and on the last three days of the Carnival. Ten choristers, dressed in the costume of pages of the time of Philip III., with plumed hats, dance a stately but most graceful measure, for about half-an-hour, within the iron screens in front of the high altar. They are dressed in blue and white for the Blessed Virgin, and in red and white for Corpus Christi. The boys accompany the minuet-like movements with the clinking of castanets. During the measure, a hymn, arranged for three voices with orchestral accompaniment, is sung in honour of the Blessed Sacrament The refrain to the verses is as follows:–

"Tu nombre Divino,
Jesus, invocamos,
Y Dios Te adoramos
"For nos encarnado,
Yen hostia abreviado
De celico pan!"

The canons of the Church of England, as well as the visitation articles of several of our bishops soon after the Reformation, afford plain proof of the not infrequent continuance of sports and feastings within the churches.

The 48th of Bishop Hoopers visitation articles runs as follows:–

"Item, that the churchwardens do not permit any buying, selling, gaming, outrageous noises, tumult, or any other idle occupying of youth, in the church, church porch, or churchyard, during the time of common prayer, sermon, or reading of the homily."

Still more explicit is the 61st article of the provincial visitation of Archbishop Grindal:–

"Whether the ministers and churchwardens have suffered any lords of misrule, or summer lords or ladies, or any disguised persons, or others, in Christmas or at May-games, or any morris-dancers, or at any other times to come, unrever-ently into the church or churchyard, and there to dance, or play any unseemly parts, with scoffs, jests, wanton gestures, or ribald talk, namely in the time of Common Prayer; and what they be that commit such disorder, or accompany or maintain them?"

The 88th Canon of the Church of England (1603), under the heading, "Churches not to be profaned," says:–

"The churchwardens or questmen, and their assistants, shall suffer no plays, feasts, banquets, suppers, church-ales, drinkings, temporal courts or leets, lay-juries, musters, or any other profane usage to be kept in the church, chapels or churchyard."

With regard to plays in churches, it has to be recollected that the mediaeval Miracle Play, particularly in England, had its origin in an elaboration of the liturgy at special seasons, in order to bring home Christian truths more closely to the understanding of an unlettered people. The primitive Passion play consisted in the solemn removal of the Crucifix on Good Friday, the laying it away beneath the altar or in a specially constructed "sepulchre," the setting of a watch to guard it and the raising it again with joyous anthem on the Resurrection morn of Easter. After the third lesson, before the Te Deum at mattins on Easter Day (according to the English use), the clergy walked in procession to the high altar, where two singingmen took the parts SS. Peter and John, whilst three altos, in albts, represented the three Maries, to each of whom certain words were assigned. The same colloquy was repeated at Mass as part of the sequence. So, too, with Nativity plays, they had their origin in the parts assigned to the choir boys and singing men, as representing angels, shepherds, wise-men, etc. A manger was always erected in one part of the church, and as the play developed a throne for Herod was placed in another position, whilst a distant corner was supposed to represent Egypt.

As the Miracle Plays grew in importance and popularity, their representation in churches became increasingly impossible, if any regard was to be had to scenic effects. Hence the actors ceased to be the clergy and choir, their place being taken by members of trade-gilds, or by wandering players. Occasionally, however, these playing troops were allowed to use the churches, of which, if space permitted, a variety of instances, many of our own culling, could be given. Nay, the authorities, both in pre-reformation and post-reformation times were occasionally lax enough to suffer secular country dramas and rude representations of historic scenes to be given by the players in the naves of the parish churches.

In the churchwardens accounts of St. Michaels, Bath, under the year 1482, are several entries pertaining to the miracle players, who doubtless performed in the church, and who certainly partook of their refreshment in the same place. The players received a preliminary refresher on their arrival, which is thus expressed in the original:–

The two best recent books on the subject are Pollards English Miracle Plays (Clarendon Press, 1890,) and Bates The English Re/igieus Drama (Macmillan, 1893.)

Propotatione le players in recordactone ludorum diver sis victims iij. d.

They seem to have been paid chiefly in kind, as the accounts are charged with–

Two bushels of corn, two dozen pots of beer, and cheese, to the value of 1. s 1. d. for the play. The wardens also paid for this play 2o. d. for skins, which would be used for disguise-ments, and 3. s. for staining diverse properties that were provided for the occasion.

Another entry relative to the same visit, has, we think, been misinterpreted by Rev. Prebendary Pearson, when he edited these accounts in 1878. The entry reads:–

Et Join Fowler pro cariando le tymbe a cimiterio dicto tempore ludi ——y. d.

Mr. Pearson thought this meant a tomb (tymba), but it is far more likely that it was a bulky platform of timber, placed in the churchyard when not in use, and only brought into the church when it was required to serve as a stage.

With regard to feasting in churches, one of the canons put forth in 1571 specially enjoined the churchwardens to disallow the holding of feasts, drinking parties, banquets, and public entertainments within the walls of churches. The Church-ales, Clark-ales, and Bid-ales, about which so much has been written, were originally held within the fabric, and a variety of other drinking and eating customs in the same place were at one time prevalent, lingering on for some time after the Reformation in certain places, and even lasting almost to our own days in occasional retired parishes.

Funeral banquets, for the entertainment of mourners, were not infrequently held in the church when the ceremony was over, or even on the next Sunday.

In Strypes edition of Stowes London it is recorded that:–

"Margaret Atkinson, widow, by her will, October 18th, 1544, orders that the next Sunday after her burial there be provided two dozens of bread, a kilderkin of ale, two gammons of bacon, three shoulders of mutton, and two couples of rabbits, desiring all the parish, as well as rich as poor, to take part thereof, and a table be set in the midst of the church, with everything necessary therto."

We have seen wills pertaining to Porlock and Cutcombe, Somersetshire, to Scropton, Derbyshire, and to Easingwold, Yorkshire, all of the latter part of the sixteenth century, which expressly provide for the refreshment of the mourners within the church.

Occasionally, too, parochial charities provided that the bequest in kind should be consumed in the church. This was the case with regard to a small seventeenth century charity, by the terms of which a certain quantity of bread and beer were to be distributed in the parish church of Barton-le-Street, Yorkshire, on Holy Thursday to the children of the parish, to be by them consumed within the church, close to the tomb of the testator. This custom prevailed until about 1820, when it was abandoned in favour of the churchyard. The reformed custom prevailed for some twenty years, when it in turn gave way to a distribution of the fund in money to the aged poor.

Sad and quaint instances of the occasional evil uses of churches in recent times, even during the present century, could be gleaned, such as cock-fighting, card-playing, etc.; but the record would be of no profit, for they would not be examples of any once established custom, but mere freaks of wanton impiety.

1bol Bap Custom.

Bv The Rev Geo. S. Tyack, B. a.

IT is not surprising that a multitude of quaint customs has sprung up around the holy days of the church. For these were the holidays of the people in " Merrie England " of the bygone times; the seasons when gossips met to talk, and young folk to play, and all the country-side was gathered first in the church, and then on the village green, or round their neighbours hospitable hearths. By sermon or by eloquent device of ritual, the parish priest endeavoured to imprint upon the simple minds of his flock the great truth which the holy day commemorated; and they, on their part, as free for the day from responsibility as from labour, showed their joy in a hundred different jests and homely sports. Within the church and without, therefore, was there ample scope for curious customs to grow up, some of which, even though the origin and meaning have been lost, live on among us to the present day.

The word feast, in the sense of a banquet, is now so familiar to us, that we are in danger of altogether forgetting that originally it contained no allusion to eating and drinking. But so universal is the idea that on all days of rejoicing a meal of special dainties should form part of the celebration, that long before we English had wrought the word into its present form, the Roman poets had begun to use its Latin original in the sense of a festal banquet. Certainly no high day is complete and national with us unless it include a dinner amongst its pleasures. We find, therefore, in surveying the holy day customs of yore, signs of much merry-making of this kind, and particularly of the dedication of special viands to certain occasions.

From time immemorial, for instance, Christmas. cheer was incomplete without its mince-pies and plum-pudding; the former emblematic, so some say, by their shape, of the manger-bed of the Infant Redeemer, and the latter by its rich ingredients of the offerings of the three kings. The pancakes of Shrove Tuesday are equally universal, and form so conspicuous a part of the days solemnities that the day is often known as " pancake-day," and the bell which formerly summoned the faithful to the shriving was similarly named the "pancake-bell." In many parts of the country, as for example at Crowle, in North Lincolnshire, the bell is still rung under that name.

Mid-Lent, or Mothering Sunday, has its peculiar fare in simnel cakes. Few days in the year have received so many titles as this one. It is Mothering Sunday from the ancient practice of priests and people going, on that day, in pilgrimage to the mother-church of the district, from which arose also a traditional habit of children visiting their parents on the same occasion. At this family re-union simnels were the proper fare. But the day is also Bragget Sunday, from the draughts of bragget, or mulled ale, with which, in some parts, notably in Lancashire, the cakes were washed down. Again it is Fag-pie Sunday, from another refection sacred to it in the same county, namely a pie of figs and spices. Refreshment Sunday, and the Sunday of the Five Loaves, have reference to the Eucharistic Gospel for the day.

The following Sunday, Passion Sunday, has its special dish in cartings, or peas fried in butter; and on Palm Sunday figs were again thought appropriate. A strange custom, existing till comparatively recent times at Sellack, in Hertfordshire, was the distribution to those present at church on Palm Sunday of buns and cider by the churchwardens, with the words, "Peace and good neighbourhood."

Even the great fast of the year has its peculiar food in the hot cross buns of Good Friday. These are probably a survival of the heathen practice of offering consecrated cakes to the gods. They were originally unleavened cakes, made, it is said, from the dough out of which the hosts for the altar were baked, a fact which suggests a connection with the Pascal regulations of the Jews. The stamp of the cross probably marks the effort of the church to give a Christian significance to a practice that was found to be practically ineradicable.

Easter, the "Queen of Festivals," has no fare so unmistakably assigned to it as some other holy days. Hare-pie is the correct thing in some places, and at Hallaton, in Leicestershire, there is an endowment for providing hare-pie, bread, and ale, for distribution at this season. At Twickenham two large cakes were formerly divided among the young folk of the parish at Easter; a harmless practice which the Puritans suppressed in 1645, with the result that often attends the efforts of busy-bodies, matters were altered for the worse; tor, thenceforward, penny loaves were purchased with the money, and flung from the Church Tower to be scrambled for. At Biddenden, in Kent, a large number of cakes and loaves are given away on this day, on the former of which is impressed the image of two females, joined together at hip and shoulder. These are the " Biddenden Maids," Eliza and Mary Chulkhurst, who are said to have been born in the village, in the year 1100, thus strangely joined, and in whose memory the rent of a plot of land, called the " Bread and Cheese Land," is thus distributed.

Other viands traditionally connected with certain holy days are the great spiced-cakes on Twelfth Night, and Valentine Buns given to children in Leicestershire, on S. Valentines Day. A special " brand" of toffee is made at Bozeat, in Northamptonshire, for S. Andrews Day; and roast goose has long been considered essential to the due observance of Michaelmas.

Reference was made above to the survival of heathen customs among us, in a dress more or less Christian; and there can be no doubt that such is the fittest description of very many holy day practices. Some usage was found in vogue, in itself harmless enough, but allied by long association with the superstitions of paganism. In some cases the mere conservatism of popular feeling kept these alive, after all meaning had died out of them; but in many instances the church took them up, and gave to the dry bones of the heathen custom a soul of Christian meaning. Conspicious among such are the use of mistletoe, and the burning of the Yule-log, as adjuncts to the gaiety and brightness of the Feast of the Nativity. Mistletoe was the most sacred of plants in the days of the Druids; and it is certainly one of the most extraordinary examples of the tenacity of life displayed by popular customs, that a tradition of special privilege should still cling to the mistletoe in spite, not only of the passage of so many centuries, but even of the exterminating wars waged against the Druids by the Romans, and against the Britons generally by the English. It was these same English forefathers of ours who taught us to burn the Yule-log in sacrifice to Thor the Thunderer.

Again, there can be little question that the " well-dressing," or decoration of springs of water with moss and flowers, so common in Derbyshire, had its origin in the worship of the nymphs or goddesses of stream and river; yet now in almost every case it has become part of the celebration of some Christian festival. At Tissington, which claims to have the only real survival of the custom, it takes place on Ascension Day; at Derby, and Wirksworth, at Whitsuntide; at Barton on the Thursday nearest to S. John the Baptists Day. A pagan rite still existing without Christian "baptism," is found in the bon-fires that yearly crown the Cornish hill-tops on the night of Midsummer Day.

Some sports and games were in the past traditionally associated with certain church festivals, for reasons which in most cases are not very clear. In Derbyshire, particularly in the county-town, and in Ashbourne, Shrove Tuesday was marked by the playing in the streets of a rough and unorganised game of football, in which a large part of the populace took part. School children were very generally supposed to have the privilege of demanding a holiday on that day, or even of enforcing one by locking the master out of the school-house. At Haxey, in North Lincolnshire, the " Haxey Hood," is always thrown on the Feast of the Epiphany. This curious sport consists in the struggle for a roll of coarse sacking, about three inches in diameter, and two feet long, known locally as the "hood," and is the occasion of much wild excitement. This is said to have no connection with the holy day, except that it is a commemoration of some local contest that chanced originally to happen on that day. A similar reason is given for the fact that the town of Stamford formerly celebrated S. Brices Day with the brutal sport of bull-running.

Other curious customs, such as the cracking of a gad-whip in Caistor Church, on Palm Sunday, by which a local land tenure was maintained, and which survived until 1846, were evidently associated, each with its special day, by a merely arbitrary arrangement, having no allusion whatever to the festival. To the same class belongs, perhaps, the ceremony of washing the tomb of Molly Grime, at Glentham, in Lincolnshire, by seven old spinsters, every Good Friday. This was regularly done until 1832, a neighbouring property being charged with the payment of one shilling each to the washers, but since that date, the tomb has been abandoned to a condition more typical of its occupants name. Another strange usage, the meaning of which it is hard to conjecture, was the pinning of bits of coloured rag to the back of the women on their way to church, on Palm Sunday, a sport once found full of amusement by the lads of Leigh, in Lancashire.

Another class of holy day usages consists of endeavours to reproduce, in some more or less realistic manner, the fact commemorated by the festival, with a result that to us seems grotesque at times, if not profane.

Amongst the more obvious of these, we must reckon the singing of carols at Christmas, a memorial of the angelic hymn heard by the shepherds at Bethlehem; and the doll laid in a decorated box, rudely representing the Holy Child in His manger-bed, which children frequently carry from door to door at that season. The miners of Llwynymaen, when asking for Christmas gifts, used at one time, it is said, to carry boards to which lighted candles were fixed, in allusion no doubt originally to the coming of the " Light of the World."

The cruel custom of stoning a wren to death on S. Stephens Day, once generally prevalent, is well-known, and was an obvious endeavour after commemorative realism. At Padstow, in Cornwall, the same. scene was enacted less objectionally on the Eve of the Conversion of S. Paul, by the stoning of a pitcher, whence that day was locally known as " Pauls Pitcher Day."

The royal offering of gold, frankincense, and myrrh, at the Chapel Royal, S. Jamess, on the Feast of the Epiphany, was once a ceremony of real dignity, but is now rather a paltry business, interesting chiefly as one of the most curious of survivals. The royal charities on Maunday Thursday, are really a portion of an otherwise lapsed custom, which recalled the action of our Lord on the day before His Crucifixion. Down to the reign of James II. the king attended by some of the great officers of his court, washed the feet of a number of poor people on this day, and then distributed money, food, and clothing among them. The lads of Kendal have a different way of keeping the day; in parties of a dozen or so, they drag, or used to drag, tin cans through the streets, beating them with sticks, until they were quite demolished. Can this, one wonders, be in any way related to that Good Friday custom of Spanish sailors, the beating and hanging in effigy of Judas the Traitor?

An old Dorset poet, Barnes, says, referring to a well-known Easter custom:

"Last Easter I put on my blue
Frock coat, the vust time, vier new;
Wi yaller buttons aal o brass,
That glittered in the zun like glass,
Bekaze twer Easter Zunday."

No good luck can attend you, so the belief was, unless you wear at least one new thing on Easter Day. The fancy probably arose from an idea of the " newness of life " of which the festival speaks to us. Easter eggs again were obviously used at first as supplying a fitting emblem of the Resurrection. As a rule they are simply treated as pretty ornaments, but at Liege, in Belgium, boys have a kind of game with them, similar to an English lads use of chestnuts, knocking two together; the boy whose egg remains unbroken the longest being proclaimed the conqueror.

The subject of holy day practices is an immense one, especially when one wanders into all the bye-paths of local peculiarities. All of them, no doubt, had their meaning in times past, and therefore their use; if some, having now become unintelligible or even foolish forms, drop year by year into disuse, we can scarcely, from mere love of the olden days, regret them. But all the more tenaciously should we cling to those old customs, which have still a living soul in them, still a lesson to teach. Our forefathers, with their ready wit in finding means for impressing truth on the mind through the medium of the eye, showed a deeper knowledge of human nature than some of their sons, who boast so freely of the superior wisdom of the nineteenth century.

Cburcb Bells: Mben ant Wlbp tbep were IRung.

By Florence Peacock.

BELLS filled a much more important place in the lives of our ancestors than they do in ours. From the time that Britain became Christian until the Reformation, there was scarcely an event in public or private history into which they did not enter–they were rung to celebrate the birth of an heir to the rich and noble, they were heard at his daughters marriage, and the marriages of his dependants; they sounded alike for high and low, rich and poor, when the soul was passing away; and again some hours after death had taken place; as well as at the funeral. On these occasions, and upon many others, it was the universal custom to ring them, but there were also what may be termed local events in honour of which they were chimed; these differed in various parts of the country; in many cases adjoining parishes followed totally different rules in this respect. Some of these customs are so quaint that they are worth recording, not only as memorials of a past that we can but dimly enter into, but as throwing considerable light upon the manners and doings of our forefathers.

As far as we are aware no complete collection of these old usages relating to the ringing of Church Bells has ever been made, though there is much valuable information to be found upon the subject in the various books upon bells which have been published during the last twenty-five years. It is said that year by year fewer bells are heard to ring upon the twenty-ninth of May, but "Oak-apple Day," as it is still called in many parts of England, is yet celebrated by the bells of Swineshead, amongst other places; and also by sprays of oak leaves being worn, though in the northern and eastern counties, if the season be a late one, it is somewhat difficult to obtain them. Some six or seven years ago many of the engines of trains running upon the Manchester, Sheffield, and Lincolnshire Railway were decked with branches of oak on that day; and it is no uncommon thing to see the plough boy adorn the heads of his horses with sprays of oak leaves in memory of King Charless escape. There is an entry in the churchwardens accounts belonging to thechurch of St. Mary at Stamford:–" 1709 Pd. Richard Hambleton for ale for the Ringers on ye 29 May. oo 06 oo." We find three years later the ringers at the church of All Saints in the same town received five shillings for ringing the bells upon the twenty-ninth of May. At Waddington it has been the custom from sometime which is now forgotten to ring one or two strokes on the tenor bell to publish the fact that an apprentice belonging to the parish is "out of his time." The fifth of November was a day of general bell-ringing all over the country, and we believe they are still sounded in many parts of England to call to mind the escape of King, Lords, and Commons from the Gunpowder Plot; Guy Fawkes is to be seen burning through the length and breadth of the land, and crackers and bonfires are usual. There is a curious inscription upon the second bell at Owmby, commemorating the events of 1605; it is dated 1687, and bears upon it:–

"LET VS REMEMBER THE 5 OF NOVEMBER."

The churchwardens accounts of S. John the Baptist at Stamford contain the following entry:– " 1608 Item paid for Rynging the vth of November vid."

In some places the bells are rung to summon people to attend the vestry meeting which is held on the Monday after Easter Sunday, to elect the churchwardens for the following term of office, to pass the church accounts for the year, and to transact various other business; this is done amongst other places at Bottesford and Epworth (the latter celebrated as being the birth-place of John Wesley, the former for possessing the most perfect specimen of an Early English church to be found in the northern part of Lincolnshire).

On Shrove Tuesday it was the general custom in pre-Reformation times to call the people to church, that they might confess their sins before Lent; this was done by one of the bells being rung, or more likely tolled, but in later times the real reason for which its sound was heard has been forgotten by the people, and where the custom has been kept up it has now got to be called " The Pancake Bell," because it is usual to have pancakes upon this day, the last of feasting, before the fast of Lent begins, and Shrove Tuesday is often known by the name of " Pancake Tuesday." This bell is rung in a great many places, though the present writer never happened to hear it: noon is the usual time for it to be heard, and at Navenby it used to be rung by the eldest apprentice in the place, but this part of the custom is now obsolete. Our forefathers believed that the ringing of church bells had the effect of allaying storms; this is illustrated by an entry in the Spalding churchwardens accounts:–"1519 Itm pd. for ryngng when the Tempest was, iijd."

In some parts of the country the bells were rung on the fifth of August to celebrate the escape of James I. from the Gowrie Plot; there are charges for ringing on this day to be found in the churchwardens accounts of Kirton-in-Lindsey at various times during the seventeenth century. In the same parish there was also the custom of ringing what is in some parts of the country known as the "Market Bell," but here it was, and we believe is still, called the "Winter Ringing," because it was only done during the months of November, December, and January, from seven until eight oclock, on Tuesday and Thursday evenings–on the former night to guide people home who had attended the Gainsborough market, and upon the latter to aid those who had been to Brigg market to find their way back again. This was a useful precaution when the country was unenclosed, as the sound of the bells told people when they were going in the right direction; the same was done in the neighbouring parish of Scotton on the Tuesday night. The custom is still kept up at Kirton-in-Lindsey during November and December, but we believe the bells are not heard upon these two evenings after Christmas, the modern idea being that the ringers are practising for that great festival of the Church.

Bells very often had names bestowed upon them; there is one in St. Marks Church, Lincoln, always spoken of as " Old Kate," and " Great Tom" of Oxford has a world-wide reputation. Many old bells have unfortunately been sold, in some cases to obtain money with which to repair the churches; in others we fear the money merely went into the pocket of the holder of the living, or those of the churchwardens; it was for the former reason that two bells at Cadney were parted with during the last century. A writer in the Gentlemaris Magazine, in 1849 (p. 158), states that there is reason to believe that, since the death of Edward VI., not less than four hundred bells have, from one cause or another, been lost in Lincolnshire alone.

In some parishes the bells are rung at the close of the morning service upon Sunday, and at Harps-well it was, until very lately, the custom to ring a bell at noon if by any chance there should be no morning service. It is popularly said, but on what authority we know not, that this bell was meant to warn those who were preparing dinner that the time for that important meal had nearly arrived. The custom of ringing a bell at the conclusion of the morning service still obtains at Kirkleatham. Inscriptions upon bells are very common, sometimes they are in English, but on the older bells it is more usual to find them in Latin. There is a bell at Alkborough which is believed to be of the early part of the fourteenth century, with the following inscription upon it:–

"Jesu For Yi Moder Sake Save All
Ye Sauls That Me Gart Make
Amen."

At Semperingham, on an early sixteenth bell, there is to be found a very useful piece of advice:–

"Be Not Ouer Busie;"

and a bell at Benniworth merely puts on record the year in which it was made:–" Anno Domini T577," it is by no means an uncommon thing to find only a date upon bells. Many of them have the names of the churchwardens for the time being, or the name of the giver of the bell or bells; at Burgh we find:–

"William Pavlin chimed so well
He payd for casting of this bell. 1589."

Most likely he was one of the ringers, but whether he gave the bell, or only paid for its recasting, we do not know. In certain parishes the bells are tolled before midnight on the thirty-first of December for the dying year; then comes a few minutes pause, and a joyous peal heralds the advent of the new year. This is done, amongst other places, at Kirton-in-Lindsey; the writer heard 1893 tolled out and 1894 ushered in with a peal on those beautiful bells; and we know that it was the custom there in 1632, for we find under that date in the churchwardens accounts:–" Item to the ringers of new yeare day mcrninge xijd." The church of this parish is dedicated to S. Andrew, and in 1658, there is an entry as follows:–" It to the ringers on St. Andrewes day o 1 o." The patron saint of Scotland seems in some parts of England to be held in high esteem; in Lincolnshire alone there are no less than sixty-eight churches dedicated to him. There is a curious tradition about the most widely known bell in Lincolnshire; it is to the effect that, when at the recasting of " Great Tom of Lincoln " in the Minster Yard, sometime during the January of 1610-11, that certain of the pious citizens determined to do all that lay in their power to make the tone of the bell as pure as possible, and therefore threw into the molten mass of metal much treasure in the form of silver tankards, spoons, and sundry other objects formed of that precious metal. That there is not the slightest truth in the story was clearly proved when the bell was once more recast in 1834, for upon a piece of the metal of which it was composed being assayed, it was found to contain a very small proportion of silver. It is strange that this belief in the power of silver to add sweetness to the tone of bells should be such a general one; we find it existing in almost all the countries of Europe, in spite of the fact that the experiment of mixing an undue proportion of this metal has always been found to impair their sound. The writer was once informed that the reason the bells of S. Martins in-the-Fields, London, are so wonderfully sweet and clear in tone is owing to the fact that Nell Gwynn, who gave them to the church, insisted upon having a quantity of silver thrown into the metal when it was fusing. Poor pretty, sinning Nell, she was religious after a manner, and she has lain in S. Martins Church upwards of two hundred years, whilst the bells she gave have sounded, and still sound, above her grave. She left a bequest to the ringers, the interest of which-was to be devoted to purchasing a leg of mutton for them to sup upon every Monday evening.

Sacring bells were, it is believed, to be found in all churches before the Reformation; they were rung to inform the congregation that the Elevation of the Host was about to take place. There is some difficulty in distinguishing between this bell and the Sanctus Bell, they seem in many cases to be the same, and in others separate. A small sacring bell was discovered in Bottesford Church (Lincolnshire) during its restoration in 1870. When the plaster was removed from the west end of the southern aisle it was seen that one of the stones in the wall was merely loosely placed in position, not built firmly in like the rest of the masonry; it was removed, and behind it, in a hole evidently made on purpose to receive it, was the bell. This bell is now in the possession of the Society of Antiquaries, and a full description of it is given in Proceedings of the Society of Antiquaries, 2nd series, vol. 5, p. 24.

There was formerly a small bell at Hemswell, named the Agnus Bell; it may perhaps have been so called by reason of its being rung at the Elevation, which was immediately followed by the singing of the Agnus Dei. The following alludes to it:–" Itm an agnus bell gone owtt of the fore sayd churche, no man knoweth how, ano dome a thowssand five hundreth three schore and fowre."

In many churches, bells and other articles were returned in 1566 as lost or missing, and no reasonable explanation of the apparently gross carelessness given. There can be but little doubt that they were secretly taken away in order that they might escape destruction; in some cases it may be that they were hidden like the bell at Bottesford, but it is probable that more often they were taken to the houses of the people who saved them; and that in after years they were lost or destroyed. Under Glenthworth, there is an entry, which seems to point to the fact that the bell was thus disposed of "A hand bell–gone, we cannot tell how, the same year," (1566).

Peacocks Church Furniture.–p. 103.

It seems to have been by no means uncommon to turn these small hand bells into mortars; we find this was done at Hemswell in 1566: " ij. hande belles, sold to Robertt Aestroppe one of the sayd churchwardens to make a mortar off."t

Queen Elizabeth ascended the throne on November i7th, 1558, S. Hughs Day, and there are many entries to be found in churchwardens accounts for ringing the bells upon that day after this date. At Kirton-in-Lindsey there is the following statement in 1581:–"Item for mending the belles aganst Sant Hew day viijd;" and then again in 1597:–" Item vpon Sante Hue daye viij." No doubt the first entry means that either the wooden framework, or else the cords of the bells needed some slight repairs; it could not have been the bells themselves. There is another entry in the Kirton-in-Lindsey accounts that is interesting, though of a somewhat later date. In 1630 we find:—Item bestowed of the ringers in ayle for Joye of the younge Prince xij." This was for ringing the bells upon the birth of Charles II.

Peacocks Church Furniture.—p. 85. Ibid.–p. 103.

In reading of these loyal payments one is reminded of the inscription upon the first bell at Witham-on-the-Hill, which evinces a very different spirit:–

"twas Not To Prosper Pride Or Hate

William Augustus Johnson Gave Me ;

But Peace And Jov To Celebrate,

And Call To Prayer To Heavn To Save Ye :

Then Keep The Terms And Eer Remember

May 29 Ye Must Not Ring

Nor Yet The Fifth Of Each November

Nor On The Crowning Of A King."

The Harvest Bell was rung in various parts of the country; at Barrow-on-Humber it was heard very early in the morning at daybreak in the eighteenth century, and then again late in the evening during the weeks of harvest. In some parishes it used to be the custom to ring a bell at eight oclock in the morning as a signal that people might then begin to glean. In the Louth churchwardens accounts, in 1556, is the following:–" To william east for knylling the bell in harvest forgathering of the pescodes iiijd." The Daily Telegraph, of 1st September, 1893, savs :– " The harvest bell is rung at the Parish Church, Driffield, at five a. m. and eight p. m. every day during harvest, the custom is a very old one."

English Belts and Belt Lote, 1888, T. North, cp. 16, p. 191.

Advent was celebrated in some places by the ringing of the bells, usually, but not invariably, in the evening; the reason for this being that the ringers were at work during the day, and therefore it could only be done when the hours of labour were ended. On S. Thomass Day the bells were often rung; and it was a very widely spread, though not a universal, custom to ring them very early on the morn of Christmas Day. In the Kirton-in-Lindsey churchwardens account we see what the ringers obtained for so doing in 1630:–" It given to the Ringers at Christenmaise day at morne xijd." The bells are, or were until lately, rung at five oclock on Christmas morning at South Kelsey. In various parts of England they were rung in a great variety of ways during Lent and upon Good Friday; on Easter Sunday, too, there has always been great divergence as to the custom of bell-ringing. The Banns Peal is still to be heard in some places; this is a peal rung after the publication of banns of marriage, it is usually chimed after morning service on the first Sunday that the banns are "put up," but this is by no means the universal practice, in some parishes it is rung on the first and third Sundays, in others on the third alone, and it varies yet again at Elsham and Searby, where it is given upon all three Sundays. Peals at Baptism are much rarer, but still there are parishes where it has been from time unknown usual to ring them. The curfew is yet to be heard in many places, though the hour varies, it being often rung at nine, and in some instances at seven oclock, instead of at eight.

In pre-Reformation times the Passing Bell, instead of being rung as it now is after death, was then really and truly a "passing-bell," for it was heard when a person was supposed to be at the point of death, in order that those in whose ears it sounded might of their charity pray for a soul so soon to be beyond human help. After the spirit had returned unto Him who gave it, the Soul Bell was rung, that the living might pray for the dead; this soul-bell, besides being rung a few hours after death, was sounded again at stated intervals, at the months end, the three months end, and so on. Surtees, the northern antiquary, alludes to this custom in the ballad of Sir John le Spring:–

"Pray for the soul of Sir John le Spring,
When the black monks sing and the chantry bells ring.
Pray for the sprite of the murdered knight,
Pray for the rest of Sir John le Spring.
And aye the mass-priest sings his song,
And patters many a prayer,
And the chantry bell tolls loud and long,
And aye the lamp burns there."

There are numerous ways of indicating the age and sex of the departed by the manner in which the passing-bell is tolled; we have been informed that in Lincolnshire alone there are between seventy and eighty different methods by which this is done.

Some few bells have upon them inscriptions showing they were meant to be rung as passing-bells. The third bell at Brant Broughton has on it:–

"Beg ye of God your soul to save
Before we call you to the grave."

It is possible that some of the customs here spoken of as now existing may recently have fallen into oblivion, but the term " existing " must only be taken to mean that it was in use at the place named when the note concerning it was made.

3nscriptions on Bells.

By William Andrews.

T T IGH up in the dusty belfry, whose grey shadows rarely see the face of man, the bells swing to and fro with unwearying zeal. But in addition to the lessons which pour from their eloquent mouths, should we scale the tall ladders of the bell tower and invade the regions of the owl and the bat, we shall find other teaching–that graven on the sides of the bells themselves–the inscriptions. Let us therefore glance over the wide field of interesting information thus presented to us. Allusions to the pitch of the bell are often the subject. A bell of Churchill, Somerset, has the following:–

Although my waiste is small
I will be heard amainst you all,
Sing on my jolly sisters.
    While Berrow, Somerset, is more brief:–
    My treble voice
Makes hearts rejoice.
    Bruton has a recast bell saying–
    Once Id a note that none could beare,
But Bilbie made me sweet and clear.
    And similarly Compton Martin–
    My sound is good that once was bad,
Letts sing my sisters and be glad.
    Badgworth, Gloucester, has a similar inscription–
    Badgworth ringers they were mad
Because Rigbe made me bad,
But Abel Rudhall you may see
Hath made me better than Rigbe.
    At Blakesley, Northamptonshire, the tenor bears– I ring to sermon with a lusty
borne,
    That all may come and none may stay at home.
    More pronounced is the self-congratulation of a bell of East Dean–
    Me melior vere,
Non est Campana sub acre, and one of Hurstpierpoint, which says– If you have a
judicious ear
    Youll own my voice is sweet and clear.
    Rye Church, in Sussex, alludes in its bells to the marriage chimes induced by the
liberality of the bridegroom– In wedlock bands, all ye who join
    With hands your hearts unite.
So shall our tuneful tongues combine
    To bless the nuptial rite.
    At other times it is the shape that is celebrated.
At Combe, Somerset, a bell says–
    My sound is good, my shape is neat,
Twas Bayley made me so compleat.
    Or the size, as at Bexhill, Sussex–
    Although I am both light and small,
I will be heard above you all."
    S. Marys, at Devizes, has another version– I am the first, altho but small,
I will be heard above you all.
    Again, names of donors are often inscribed upon bells, and these are handed down
to us from very early dates; or sometimes the fact of subscription is mentioned in
general terms of gratitude. So Bagborough, Somerset, says–
    Bouth owld and young did agree full well
To pay for casting of this bell,
Because a true tale it should tell.

And Bath Abbey has a very terse bell couplet,
All you of Bath that heare mee sound
Thank Lady Hoptons hundred pound.

A Devon bell has–
Squire Arundel the great my whole expense did raise,
Nor shall our tongues abate to celebrate his praise.

These hints, or downright references on bells to the pecuniary means of their erection, may be supplemented by the inscription at Buxted, which promises as follows–
At proper times my voice Ill raise
And sound to my subscribers praise.

But in the last two centuries such expressions of gratitude for subscriptions to casting or re-casting are common enough. So in a similar strain speaks the bell of Alderton, Im given here to make a peal
And sound the praise of Mary Neale.

At Binstead, too, a bell says
Dr. Nicholas gave five pound
To help cast this peal tuneable and sound.

Bells at first bore strictly religious inscriptions; afterwards that rule became more relaxed, and irrelevant matters often find expression. After 1600 the claims of religion to be alone regarded on bells may be said to be almost entirely passed over. Marlboroughs victories are commemorated on the bells of S. Helens, Worcester, and those of Ottery and S. Martin, Exeter, have medals on which are represented grotesque pieces levelled at the churchmen in the most approved style of mediaeval satire. Sometimes, nay, most often. the poetical attempts in the inscriptions are, to say the least, somewhat wanting in an indefinite something that goes to make true poetry. Yet the simple appeals of some of them do not fall unregarded. So when rich men give bells we find such an inscription as this–
Of your charite prai for the soulles of John Slutter, John Hunt, and Willem Slutter.

An instance has been given of historical events being inscribed upon bells. A further one is that of the bell of Ashover, Derbyshire, which upon re-casting was inscribed–
This old bell rung the downfall of Buonaparte and broke, April, 1814.

At Tadcaster it is recorded on the fifth bell– It is remarkable that these bells were moulded in the great frost, 1783. C. and R. Dalton, Fownders, York.

An extremely curious inscription appears on a bell at Pucknowle, Dorsetshire, dated 1629. It reads without stop or space–
Hethatvillpvrchashonovrsgaynemvstancientlatherstilmayn-tayne.

"Lather" is an old English term meaning " to make a noise." A bell at Lichfield, which was destroyed in 1652, bore the following:– I am ye bell of Jesus, and Edward is our King,
Sir Thomas Heywood first caused me to ring.

Many inscriptions on bells are, or contain, allusions to the vigilance of monastic times. Such is one at Ashill, Somerset, which simply says– I call to wake you all.

As pithy an inscription appears on the bell of S. Ives, which is rung early in the morning.

It is–

Arise, and go about your business.

A Coventry bell, dated 1675, says– I ring at six to let men know

When too and fro their worke to goe.

Patriotic expressions are common; among such is

Brusford,

Come let us ring

For Church and King.

And Hurstpierpoint,

Ye people all who hear us ring

Be faithful to your God and King.

Sometimes a whole set of bells bore inscriptions which may be read continuously. An instance is at S. Marys, Ticehurst, where the bells have– 1. I am she that leads the van, Then follow me now if you can.

2. Then I speak next, I can you tell,

So give me rope and ring me well.

3. Now I am third, as I suppose,

Mark well now time and fourth close.

4. As I am fourth, I will explain If youll keep time youll credit gain.

5. Now I am fifth, as I suppose,

Then ring me well and tenor close.

6. This is to show for ages yet to come

That by subscription we were cast and hung

And Edward Lulham is his name

That was the actor of the same.

Northfield bells, Worcestershire, give an account of the contest in the vestry-room which led to the completion of the peal– 1. Though once but five we now are six.

2. And gainst our casting some did strive.

3. But when a day of meeting there was fixed.

4. Appeared nine gainst twenty-six.

5. It was Wm. Kettle that did contrive

To make us six that were but five.

Another bell bears the date and churchwardens names. At Coventry on a. peal of bells, cast in 1774, are the following inscriptions– 1. Though I am but light and small I will be heard above you all.

2. If you have a judicious ear

You will own my voice both sweet and clear.

3. Such wondrous power to music given,

It elevates the soul to heaven.

4. Whilst thus we join in cheerful sound,

May love and loyalty abound.

5. To honour both God and King

Our voices shall in concert ring.

6. Music is medicine to the mind.

7. Ye ringers all that prize
Your health and happiness,
Be sober, merry, wise,
And youll the same possess.

8. Ye people all who hear me ring
Be faithful to your God and King.

9. In wedlocks bands all ye who join
With hands your hearts unite:
So shall our tuneful tongues combine
To laud the nuptial rite.

10. I am and have been called the common bell
To ring when fire breaks out to tell.

On the bells of S. Peters, Nottingham, the appended lines appear:–
Our voices shall with joyful sound
Make hills and valleys echo round.

We celebrate th auspicious morn
On which the Son of God was born.

Our voices shall in concert ring
To honour God and King.

The bride and groom we greet in holy wedlock joind,
Our sounds are emblems of hearts in love combined.

I toll the funeral knell, I hail the festal day.–
The fleeting hour I tell, I summon all to pray.

The longest continuous bell inscriptions we have noted are from Bakewell, Derbyshire, and on a peal of eight bells. They run thus:– 1. When I begin Our merry Din,
This Band I lead from Discord Free;
And for the Fame of human Name,
May evry Leader copy Me.

2. Mankind like Us, too oft are found
Possessd of Nought but empty Sound.

3. When of departed Hours We toll the Knell, Instruction take and spend the future well.

4. When Men in Hymens Bands unite,
Our Merry Peals produce Delight;
But when Death goes his dreary Rounds,
We send forth sad and solemn Sounds.

5. Thro Grandsires and Tripples with Pleasure men range, Till Death calls the Bob and brings on the Last Change.

6. When Victry crowns the Public Weal With Glee We give the merry Peal.

7. Would Men Like Us join and agree
Theyd live in tunefull Harmony.

8. Possessd of deep sonorous Tone
This Belfry Ki.: g sits on his Throne;

And, when the merry Bells go round,
Adds to and mellows evry Sound;
So in a just and well poisd State,
Where all Degrees possess due Weight,
One greater Powr, One greater Tone
Is ceded to improve their own.

During a recent visit to Bakewell church we copied an epitaph blending in a remarkable degree business, loyalty and religion:–

To the Memory of
Matthew Strutt.

Of this town, farmer, long famed in these parts for veterinary skill. A good neighbour, and a staunch friend to Church and King. Being churchwarden at the time the present peal of bells were hung. Through zeal of the House of God, and unremitting attention to the airy business of the belfry he caught a cold, which terminated his existence May 25, 1798, in the 68 year of his age.

A beautiful Latin inscription has one–a Rutland bell–

Non clamor sed amor cantat in aure dei, i. e., It is not noise, but love that sings in the ear of God.

And it is in the same county that we find the modern use of the death-bell described, I sound not for the souls of the dead but the ears of the living.

Cheltenham, too, bears out the spirit of this inscription in the following:– I to prayer the living do combine
The dead shall hear a greater sound than mine.

The offices of the various bells form a large proportion of their legends, particularly those uses which are the most common. Thus the death bell at Axbridge, Somerset, states,

For homesoever this bell doth toll
The Lord have mercy on that sole!

Many Somersetshire bells have the following and similar inscriptions:– I to the church the living call,
And to the grave I summon all.

Brent, Somerset, has a bell with–
When I doth toll pray mind your souls
And in God put your trust,
As may be well with you at last
When you come to doust.

And Backwell, in the same county– I sound to bid the sick repent, In hopes of life when breath is spent.

A bell at Stratton, Cornwall, is shorter–
I call the quick to church and dead to grave.

A bell in Ghent describes the purposes for which it was used: it is not an uncommon form in the Netherlands. Translated it reads:–

My name is Roelant;
When I toll it is for a fire,
When I swing then there is storm in Flanders.

Religious sentiments and quotations are found in thousands on bells old and new. Such are–Te deum Laudamus.

On the bell at Peterborough Cathedral

Venite Exultemus Domino. In Westminster Abbey

Christie audi nos.

Sometimes a letter of the inscription is found inverted; rarely a whole word. Such, however, is the case at Clapham, in Bedfordshire, where the line runs–

God save the ipjniq

The prayers for the dead mark the religious changes of the country, and not less the invocations to the saints, which form one branch of bell lore. Elstead has a bell inscribed–

Sancta Paule, ora pro nobis.

Washington, in Sussex, one bearing–

O Sancte Stephane.

And Balcombe, in the same county, one–

Vox Augustini Sonat in aure Dei.

The uses to which bells were dedicated may be further exampled from their inscriptions. S. Michael, Coventry, has a bell bearing– I am, and have been called the common bell

To ring when fire breaks out to tell.

And at Sherborne, in Dorsetshire, dated 1652, a bell piously says–

Lord, quench this furious flame,

Arise, run, help put out the same.

We may here appropriately conclude with some lines inscribed upon the tower of Batley Church, Yorkshire, in memory of a former set of bells:

"The Requiem of the late three bells of Batley Church, two of which were introduced into the tower in the 17th century, and the third or last in the 18th century, and were taken down in the 1pth century, at the close of the year of our Lord 1851, bearing the following respective dates and inscriptions, viz., upon the middle bell: Tho. Deighton G. O. 1658; largest bell, 1684 Gloria in Altissimis Deo. Ric. Mann, Churchwarden; last and least bell, Dalton of York fecit 1791. To Father, Son, and Holy Ghost Eternal glory raise.

"Author of the following lines, Mr. Luke Blakeley, of Upper Batley; third of that name in the family, and nephew of Mr. Luke Blakeley of the same place, who died Jan. 17th, in the year of our Lord 1836, and was interred in Batley Churchyard.

"One hundred years, yea almost two,

Weve hung in that turret grey,

And many changes we have seen

As time has fled away

We seen the bride and bridegroom gay,

Weve chimed their joy to tell;

Alas! before the day has closd

Weve tolld the funeral knell.

Weve merrily rung for victories gaind

Oer Britains enemies;
Then mourned for the brave who bled
    To gain those victories.
    Weve highly lauded pomp and power,
Then calld on men to pray,
    A requiem rung with the weeping and sad,
Then revelld with the gay.
    Weve seen the scourge of civil war
Approach where we have stood.
    Weve seen oppressions cruel hand
Reeking with kindred blood.
    Our solemn tolling for the dead
Falls on the mourners ear,
    Then the bereavd and aching heart
Feels desolate and drear.
    Dirges weve rung for Kings and Queens
As they to the tomb went down,
    Then joyfully welcomd the heir
Who came to wear the crown.
    We saw the star of Brunswick rise
And beam upon our strand,
    We see its full refulgent ray
Illumine this happy land.
    Victoria the sceptre sways,
    And bright her virtues shine,
Long may she live, long may she reign
    Best of her royal line.
    We joyfully haild her natal day,
    We haild her to the throne,
We blithely haild her nuptial hour,
    For her we neer shall moan.
    Were taken from that turret grey
    Where we for long have hung,
Like worn out lumber thrown away,
    Forever mute, each tongue.
    And now our changes all are rung
    Here ends our dying song;
Our last our final peal is done:
    Farewell! Farewell! Ding Dong."

Ai the bottom of the plate occurs the name of the engravers, Sellers and Nelson, Leeds.

laws ot the 3Bclfi.

By William Andrews.

THE ringing chambers of many old churches contain curious rules in poetry and prose for regulating the conduct of the ringer and the visitor. Some of the orders are extremely quaint, and all appear framed as a ready means of obtaining money in fines to be spent in beer. In bygone times there appears to have been a close connection between the belfry and the cellar. One of the best examples which has come under our notice is from Hathersage, Derbyshire, and dates back to about 1660:–

You gentlemen that here wish to ring,
See that these laws you keep in every thing;
Or else be sure you must without delay,
The penalty thereof to the ringers pay.

First, when you do into the bell-house come,
Look if the ringers have convenient room;
For if you do be an hindrance unto them,
Fourpence you forfeit unto these gentlemen.

Next if you do here intend to ring,-
With hat or spur, do not touch a string;
For if you do, your forfeit is for that,
Just fourpence down to pay, or lose your hat.
If you a bell turn over, without delay,
Fourpence unto the ringers you must pay;
Or if you strike, misscall, or do abuse,
You must pay fourpence for the ringers use.

For every oath here sworn, ere you go hence,
Unto the poor then you must pay twelvepence;
And if that you desire to be enrolled
A ringer here, these words keep and hold!

But whoso doth these orders disobey,
Unto the stocks we will take him straightway,
There to remain until he be willing
To pay his forfeit and the clerk a shilling.

A similar set of rules were adopted at Chapel-en-le-Frith, in the same county.
The following quaint lines are from St. Peters, Shaftesbury:–

What musick is there that compard may be
To well-tuned bells enchanting melody?
Breaking with their sweet sounds the willing air,
They in the listning ear the soul ensnare,
When bells ring round and in their order be,
They do denote how neighbours should agree;
But if they clam the harsh sound spoils the sport,
And tis like women keeping Dover Court.
Of all the music that is played or sung
Theres none like bells, if they are well rung.
Then ring your bell–well if you can,
Silence is best for evry man;
In your ringing make no demur,
Pull off your hat, your belt, and spur;
And if your bell you overset

The ringers fee you must expect!
Fourpence you are to pay for that.
But that if you do swear or curse,
Twelvepence is due, pooll out your purse,
Our laws are old, they are not new,
Both clerk and ringers claim their due.

We have from Tong, Salop, the following curious dated example:– If that to ring
you do come here,
You must ring well with hand and ear;
Keep stroke of time and go not out,
Or else you forfeit, out of doubt.
Our law is so constructed here,
For evry fault a jugg of beer.
If that you ring with spur or hat,
A jugg of beer must pay for that.
If that you take a rope in hand,
These forfeits you may not withstand.
Or, if that you a bell oerthrow,
It will cost sixpence ere you goe.
If in this place you swear or curse,
Sixpence you pay–out with your purse.
Come! pay the clerk, it is his fee,
For one that swears shall not go free.
These laws are old, and are not new,
Therefore the clerk must have his due.

George Harrison, 1694.

From the belfry of Dunster, Somersetshire, are the following lines:–
You that in ringing take delight,
Be pleased to draw near;
These articles you must observe
If you mean to ring here.
And first, if any overturn
A bell, as that he may,
He forthwith for that only fault In beer shall sixpence pay.
If anyone shall curse or swear
When come within the door,
He then shall forfeit for that fault
As mentioned before.
If anyone shall wear his hat
When he is ringing here
He straightway then shall sixpence pay In cyder or in beer.
If anyone these articles
Refuseth to obey,
Let him have nine strokes of the rope,
And so depart away.

The foregoing bears the date of 1787. We have a shorter set of orders from Bowden:–

You ringers all, observe these orders well!
He pays his sixpence that oerturns a bell;
And he that rings with either spur or hat,
Must pay his sixpence certainly for that;
And he that rings and does disturb ye peal,
Must pay his sixpence or a gun of ale.
These laws elsewhere, in evry church are used,
That bell and ringers may not be abused.

It is stated in Halliwells " Dictionary of Archaisms and Provincialisms" gun is a North country word for a large flagon of ale.

From All Saints Church, Hastings, we have the following lines:– I. H. S.

This is a belfry that is free
For all those that civil be;
And if you please to chime or ring
It is a very pleasant thing.

There is no musick playd or sung,
Like unto bells when theyre well rung;
Then ring your bells well, if you can,
Silence is the best for every man.

But if you ring in spur or hat,
Sixpence you pay, be sure of that;
And if a bell you overthrow,
Pray pay a groat before you go.–1756.

Similar verses to the foregoing we have seen in several places. From the parish church at Grantham we have the following example,, dating back to about the middle of the last century:–

He that in Ringing takes delight,
And to this place draws near,
These Articles set in his sight
Must keep if he Rings here.
The first he must observe with care
Who comes within the door, Must if he chance to curse or swear,
Pay Sixpence to the poor.
And whosoeer a noise does make,
Or idle story tells,
Must Sixpence to the Ringers take
For melting of the Bells.
If any like to smoke or drink,
They must not do so here, Good reason why–just let them think
This is Gods House of Prayer.
Young men that come to see and try,
And do not Ringing use,
Must Six Pence give the company,

And that shall them excuse.
So that his hat ons head does keep,
Within this sacred place, Must pay his Six Pence ere he sleep;
Or turn out with disgrace.
If any one with spurs tos heels
Ring here at any time,
He must, for breaking articles,
Pay Six Pence for his crime.
If any overthrow a Bell,
As that by chance he may, Because he minds not Ringing well,
He must his Six Pence pay.
Or if a noble minded man
Come here to Ring a bell, A Shilling is the Sextons fee,
Who keeps the church so well
At any should our Parson sneer,
Or Wardens rules deride,
It is a rule of old most clear
That such shant here abide.
The Sabbath-day we wish to keep,
And come to church to pray;
The man who breaks this ancient rule
Shall never share our pay.
And when the bells are down and ceased, It should be said or sung,
May God preserve the Church and King,
And guide us safely home.

In September, 1875, we visited Holy Trinity Church, Hull, to ascertain if any Ringers Regulations were to be found in the church. We learned, on enquiry, a number of quaint orders were hung up in the ringing chamber some years ago, but a mischievous boy mutilated them with a knife, so that they were taken down. The person in charge, however, kindly submitted for our inspection the disfigured orders, and after considerable trouble, we were able to make a transcript which, we think, will prove interesting:–

Orders.

Agreed upon by the sexton and ringers of the Holy Trinity Church, Kingston-upon-Hull, approved of and allowed by the Rev. William Mason, vicar, Mr. George Maddison, and Mr. Thomas Bell, churchwardens, of the same church, the first day of May, Anno Domini 1730, and confirmed by the Rev. John Healey Bromby, vicar, Thomas Mitchell, and Charles Anthy. Forrester, churchwardens, the first day of May, 1838.

It is ordered, that every person who shall ring any bell with hat or spurs on, shall forfeit and pay sixpence for the use of the ringers.

It is ordered, that every person who shall pull any bell from off her stay and cannot set her again, shall forfeit and pay for use aforesaid, one shilling.

It is ordered, that every person who shall throw any bell over, shall forfeit and pay for the use aforesaid, sixpence, and over and above this in case anything be broken by such overthrow, such person shall also pay the charge of repairing the same again.

It is ordered, that every person so soon as he has set his bell shall immediately hank up the strop or rope, or in default thereof shall forfeit and pay for use aforesaid, sixpence.

It is ordered, that if any person shall untruss himself upon the lead in any part, or cut and mark the same with a knife or any other thing, such offender shall forfeit and pay for the use aforesaid, sixpence.

It is ordered, that any person who shall have read any of these orders with his hat upon his head shall forfeit and pay for the said use, sixpence.

Next appears the names of the vicar, churchwardens, ringers, who held office in 1730, and a similar list is given for 1838, when the above orders were reprinted at the expense of Mr. W. Green, a sidesman.

The following "Articles and Orders to be Observed by Ringers " at Stow, in the county of Lincoln, were written by William Swift, schoolmaster, and used to hang in the ringing chamber of the church:–

All you who hath a mind to Learn to Ring s. d.
Must to the sexton Admission Money bring. 2 6
These Articles observed strict must be,
Or your expelled this society.
Two Nights a Week, Sirs, you must meet, or pay
This Forfeiture to us without delay, o 2
Or when the Sexton for you tolls a bell
You must appear, or else this Forfeit tell. o 2
And when you come upon this Belfry If that you noise or talk, this forfeit pay, o 1
When you Round peals can Ring, you must pay down
To be a change man, Sirs, Just half-a-crown, 2 6
On the first change that you have Learned to Ring,
One shilling more must pay, Sirs, thats the thing, I o
And every Ringer must spend more or Less,
As he thinks meet, to wish you good Success, o 2 If you would learn to prick a peal in score,
Unto these College youths you must pay more. 1 o
When you know Bob, Hunt, Single Dodge compleat
Youll not deny our College youths a treat, 2 6
On our Feast-Day, the Twenty-ninth of May,
Each member must, Sirs, just one shilling pay, 1 o
When our accompts are passed, Sirs, for Truth,
And you are stiled a College youth,
New Stewards then are chose, and by and by If that you do the Stewardship deny,
Your fine must pay–as in the margin see, 1 6
Then from your Stewardship one year are free.
These Rules peruse well before you enter, Its a hard task on which you venture.
When once a member you are freely made,

These Articles must justly be obeyd.

So now, my Lads, admission money bring, 2 6

And we will Learn you presently to ring.

John Marshall, William Smith,

Master. Notary.

March 1st, 1770.

The following on a card was also placed in the belfry of Stow Church:–

We ring the quick to church, the dead to grave,

Good is our use, such usage let us have.

Who swears or curses, or in cholric mood

Quarrels or strikes, although he draws no blood,

Who wears his hat, or overturns a bell,

Or by unskilful handling mars a peal,

I et him pay sixpence for each single crime,

Twill make him cautious gainst another time.

So, when the bells are ceased, then let us sing

God bless our Holy Church–God save the Queen.

The foregoing are a few examples of the many curious ringers regulations which found a place in belfrys in bygone times. Mr. J. Potter Briscoe, in his " Curiosities of the Belfry" (London, 1883), gives a complete collection of these old-time rules in prose and poetry.

By Isaac J. Reeve.

THE old time belfry laws were the means of many persons being fined, and the money so obtained was spent in ale. Ringers Jugs were by no means uncommon, and some were curious examples of the potters art.

There is a curious jug or pitcher belonging to the ringers of Hadleig"h. It is a " vas ansatum " having two ears, is circular in shape, swelling out in the middle, and being more contracted at the ends. It is brown earthenware glazed. It holds sixteen quarts, and bears this inscription, very rudely indented, apparently with a chisel when the clay was soft, the first word ME, or perhaps M. E. I., is in italics, the rest in Roman capitals:—

Me, Thomas Windle, Isaac Bunn, John Mann, Adam Sage, George Bond, Thomas Goldsborough. Robert Smith, Henry West. (No doubt the names of the eight ringers.)

Below the names,– If you love me doe not lend me,

Euse me often and keep me clenly,

Fill me full or not at all, If it be strong, and not with small.

Below all, in the front, is the word Hadly, underneath one handle is the date, 17 F. G. 15, and under the other, 17 R. O. 15, the letters probably the initials of the potters. The jug is in the possession of Mr. Pettitt, of the Eight Bells Inn, who holds it for the ringers, of whom he is the leader. It is still occasionally used on the occasion of any profitable wedding, and filled every Christmas by mine host, when the ringers assemble for a frolic, with strong beer, which goes by the name of old King William, and strangers going in are expected to pay sixpence to assist in keeping it full, according to its own request.

The ringers1 pot–a brown glazed jug with handle, holding about two gallons–having the following inscription in rude letters–

Here you may see what
I request of Hanst (honest) Gentlemen
My Baly (belly) filed of the Bast I com
But now and then, 1716, was formerly carried from house to house by the bell-ringers of Ixworth, in Suffolk, to receive whatever beer the liberal parishioners might be disposed to bestow. It has been disused about thirty years. It was probably made at the celebrated pottery in the neighbouring parish of Wattisfield. A similar kind of jug, both in shape and size, to that of Hadleigh, belongs to the ringers of Clare. On one side is a crown in faint relief, under that a bell in large proportion, and on it impressed in italics:–

Campane
Sonant canore.

Beneath the clapper is this,–
Clare Ringers,
1729.

Near the base there is an aperture for a tap to draw off the beer, there being no spout or lip.

At Hinderclay, in Suffolk, is a ringers pitcher, still preserved in the church tower, of form and size similar to the Hadleigh jug: it is thus inscribed:–

By Samuel Moss this pitcher was given to the noble society of ringers, at Hinderclay, viz., Tho. Sturgeon, Ed. Lock, John Haws, Ric. Ruddock, and Relf Chapman, to which society he once belonged, and left in the year 1702.

From London I was sent
As plainly doth appear,
It was to this intent–
To be filled with strong beer.
Pray remember the pitcher when empty.

A similar pitcher is in the adjoining church tower of Garboldisham, Norfolk.

At the Mackworth Arms, at Swansea, a similar kind of jug may be seen in a niche on the staircase, but the colour is light yellow, and the workmanship of a superior order, it has but one handle, and the following inscription in two lines:–

Come fill me well with liquor sweet, and that is good when friends do meet, When I am full then drink about, I neer will fail till all is out.

Underneath were representations of flowers, birds, and fishes.

There is in the Norfolk and Norwich Museum a large jug, which was presented in July, 1831, by the Rev. G. R. Leathes, of Shrophan. It is of brown earth, glazed, dated 1676, and inscribed:–

John Wayman,
J. F.

Come Brother, shall we join?
Give me your twopence–here is mine.

This most likely belonged to a company of Shrophan ringers. It has but one handle, and is rather curiously ornamented.

Note.–This article was written about twenty-five years ago.— Editor.

Customs airt Superstitions of Baptism.

By The Rev. Canon Benham, B. d., F. s. a.

THE present paper is, of course, in no sense a discussion of the doctrine of Christian Baptism. The names by which this Sacrament has been called, however, express, to some degree, the views which have been taken of it in the Christian Church, and these names must be briefly recounted. One of the earliest titles was Indul-gentia, " remission of sin." This is a title as old as the third century, and the idea has found expression in the Nicene Creed. Palingenesia, "new birth," is an expression equally old. It will be remembered that one of the earliest symbolical names of our Lord Jesus Christ was Ickthus, "Fish;" it is found on the walls of the Roman Catacombs. Now this is really an acrostic, the letters which made it up are the initial letters of the sentence, "Jesus Christ, Son of God, our Saviour," and Tertullian, the first writer of the Latin Church, says, "We are fishes, born in water, conformable to the name of our Lord Jesus Christ, Ichthus." Justin Martyr (middle of the second century) speaks of the baptismal water as " the water of life," and Cassiodorus (fifth century) calls itfons divinus, "the divine fountain," whence comes our name " Font." S. Chrysostom and other Greek fathers use the name " Illumination," (Photismos,) and S. Augustine calls it Salus, "Salvation," as he calls the Lords Supper " Life." Another word was Sphragis, "Seal," because it was the seal of a covenant made between God and man. This title is as old as the second century. The same idea is conveyed in Augustines expression, Character Dominicus, "the Divine, i. e., stamp mark."

Baptism was rejected by some of the early heretics, chiefly by the Gnostics, who asserted that all religion lay in knowledge, and under pretence of exalting spiritual worship, would admit of no external or corporeal symbols whatsoever, and also by the Manichaeans, who, holding that all matter is in itself evil, consistently rejected the religious use of water. Some early heretics also objected to the use of water only, asserting that this was no better than the baptism of John, whereas our Lord was to baptize also with fire, and they seem, while baptizing with water, to have also touched the ears with fire. Others, by some chemical art, created an appearance of fire on the surface of the water. (Bingham, iii. 414.)

But to come down to later times, there are curious records which tell how the matter used in the Baptismal rite was not always water as it is with us. A letter of Pope Gregory to Archbishop Sigurd of Norway (a. d. 1241) says " Forasmuch as we learnt from you, that it is sometimes the custom, on account of the want of water, for infants in your country to be baptized in ale, we hereby decree that as according to the Gospel Doctrine, it is necessary that they be born of water and of the Holy Spirit, they ought not to be accounted as baptized who are baptized in ale." And there are Bulls and decrees of Councils to the same effect. In Notes and Queries (ii. 5, 524) is a quotation from an unpublished diary of the sixteenth century, telling how "at Presume, Aug. 30, 1574, one Griffith ap Bedo Du, which dwelt at Pilleth, at the christening of his son would not have the same to be christened as the manner is, in water, but upon a proud stomach caused the water to be voided out of the font, and filled it with wine, and so caused his son to be therein christened." And the diarist goes on to say that all the country round noted from that time that "he" and his continued to grow to decay in substance and credit until his race was extinguished."

Controversies concerning Infant Baptism, as well as concerning Immersion as distinguished from affusion, or pouring water upon the baptized, would be out of place here. The latter practice, rendered necessary in our northern climate, has led to the use of the font. Nevertheless, baptism by immersion is not unknown in the Church of England. Under the Church of S. Lawrence, Reading, there is a baptistery under the pews, and in 1866, these pews were temporarily removed and a family of Quakers were baptized in it. At Trinity Church, Marylebone and at Scarborough, there are records within the last few years of adults baptized by immersion. In the parish church of Cranbrook, in the Weald of Kent, is a curious bath for immersion, of which the following is the history. John Johnson, who was Vicar there at the end of the seventeenth century, found on entering upon the incumbency that there were many of his parishioners who were unbaptized, and who, though they were desirous of attending his ministry, were in favour of being baptized by immersion. The Anabaptists were strong in that district during the Commonwealth. He therefore resolved to meet their views. There was a flight of steps leading up, on the inside, into the Parvise or room over the southern porch. At the top of of these steps, on the landing so to speak, he constructed a deep bath, reaching down in fact to the floor of the church, so that the minister could take the person to be baptized up the steps and there immerse him. This charitable concession to the convictions of his people is still to be seen. I believe, however, that there are only two records of it having been used since its erection. Similar baptisteries are to be seen at Ebbw Vale, Aberdare, and elsewhere.

The Canons of the Church order that the font shall be of stone. In some churches may still be seen a small vessel of plaster or earthenware, in which a little water is put for baptism, so as to save filling the font. But it is illegal, and is now rarely seen. Bishop Wilberforce, wherever he found them on Visitations, ordered their removal. In the case of private baptisms, some clergy keep a basin which they carry with them, similarly to a pocket Communion set, and use it for no other purpose. And this certainly seems the more reverent method. Others however use any basin which may be handy, and then send it back to its ordinary use with a view to prevent any feeling of superstition. It seems from the following passage in Pepyss diary, that the clergy were in the habit of performing public as well as private baptisms in private houses:–

"Lords Day. My wife and I to Mr. Martins where I find the company almost all come to the christening of Mrs. Martins child, a girl. After sitting long, till the church was done, the parson comes and then we to christen the child. After the christening comes in the wine and sweetmeats, etc."

A statute dating from the time of Henry III. runs as follows:–"If really from necessity the child shall be baptized at home, the water on account of the sanctity of baptism shall either be poured into the fire, or carried away to the church to be poured. into the Baptistery and the vessel shall be burnt at the same time, or shall be deputed to the use of the Church."

One of the most confessedly difficult passages in the New Testament is S. Pauls question, "What shall they do who are baptized for the dead? If the dead are not raised at all, why then are they baptized for them?" (1 Cor. xv. 29). Bingham discusses this text at some length. Two main lines of interpretation have been followed by the various commentators. The one is, that there was a custom among some of the early heretics, that when anyone died without baptism, another was baptized in his stead. S. Chrysostom says that this was practised among the Marcionites with a great deal of ridiculous ceremony, which he thus describes:–" After any catechumen was dead, they hid a living man under the bed of the deceased, then, coming to the dead man, they spake to him and asked him whether he would receive baptism? And he making no answer, the other answered for him, and said, He would be baptized in his stead. And so they baptized the living for the dead, as if they were acting a comedy upon the stage; so great was the power of Satan in the minds of these vain men. Afterward, when anyone challenged them upon this practice, they had the confidence to plead the apostles authority for it." Bingham proceeds to reject this interpretation on two grounds; 1st, that it was superstitious and delusive, "Any Jew or Gentile might easily be made a Christian by having another, after his death, baptized for him." This objection, however, is not conclusive, it does not follow that S. Paul approved of the practice, no doubt he would account it a superstition. But he is employing the argiimentum ad hominem. " What do these people mean by their practice if they do not believe in a resurrection?" The second objection is more cogent, viz.: that the interpretation in question was not accepted by any early Christian writer.

The other line of interpretation which Bingham adopts, shall be given in his own words. " But S. Chrysostom gives a much more rational account of the apostles argument, for he supposes him to refer to the Catholic custom, of making every cate-chumen at his own baptism, with his own mouth declare his belief of the resurrection of the dead by repeating the creed of which that was a part, and so being baptized into that faith, or hope of the resurrection of the dead. And, therefore, he puts them in mind of this saying, If there be no resurrection of the dead, why art thou then baptized for the dead, that is, the body? For, therefore, thou art baptized for the dead, believing the resurrection of the dead, that the body may not remain dead, but revive again. So that baptizing for the dead, is an elliptical expression for being baptized into the faith or belief of the resurrection of the dead. And so I think Tertullian is to be understood when he says in opposition to the error of the Marcionites, "That to be baptized for the dead is to be baptized for the body, which is declared to be dead by baptism;–that is, we are baptized into the belief of the resurrection of the body, both whose death and resurrection are represented in baptism." And the interpretation of Epiphanius comes pretty near these, when he says, "It refers to those who were baptised upon the approach of death, in the hopes of the resurrection from the dead; for they shewed thereby that the dead should rise again, and that therefore they had need of the remission of sins, which is obtained in baptism." The same sense is given by Theodoret, and Theophylact, and Balsamon, and Zonaras, and Matthew Blastaras among the Greeks; and it is embraced by Bishop Patrick, and Dr. Hammond, as the most natural and genuine exposition of this difficult passage of the apostle."

The use of Sponsors in the administration of baptism dates from the earliest times. Their duties varied according as the baptized person were an infant or an adult. For the most part at first, parents were sponsors for their own children, and it was the exception when they were not.

"The extraordinary cases," says Bingham, " in which the baptized were presented by others were commonly such cases where the parent could not, or would not, do that kind office for them; as when slaves were presented to baptism by their masters; or children when parents were dead, brought by the charity of any who would show mercy on them; or children exposed by their parents, which were sometimes taken up by the holy virgins of the church "(iii. 552.) Sponsors for children were called on, 1st, to answer in their name to all the interrogatories of baptism; 2nd, to be guardian of their spiritual life for the future In the case of adults their duty was to admonish and instruct them both before and after baptism. Very commonly sponsors for adults were deacons or deaconesses. Only one sponsor originally was required, in the case of adults, a man for a man and a woman for a woman. For children there was no restriction as to the sex of the sponsor.

Sponsors were called " spiritual parents," and out of this relationship grew the practice in the Roman Catholic Church, which forbade sponsors, or godparents, from marrying within the forbidden degrees of spiritual relation. The first notice of this occurs in the laws of Justinian, which forbid a man to marry a woman, whether she be slave or free, to whom he has stood godfather, " because nothing induces a more parental affection, or juster prohibition of marriage, than this tie, by which their souls are in a divine manner, united together." This was afterwards extended to prohibition between a godfather and the mother of the child, and the prohibition took final shape in the decrees of Trent, which further forbid marriages between the sponsors themselves, nor may the baptizer marry the baptized. A host of troubles and difficulties are on record in the pages of history, arising out of these prohibitions.

It is uncertain when proxies were first allowed. The first English record appears to be the case of Jane, the daughter of Thomas Godfrey, of Grub Street, who was baptized at S. Giles, Cripplegate, in 1615. Mr. Godfrey kept a diary, in which he writes, "My gossips were Mrs. Jane Hallsye, wife of Mr. John Hallsye, one of the Citty Captains, and my sister Howlt, and Sir Multon Lombard, who sent Mr. Michael Lee for his deputy. My brother Thomas Isles afterwards bestowed a christening sermon on us."

In mediaeval times a child on being baptized was arrayed by the priest in a white robe, which had been anointed with sacred oil, and was called a Chrismale. This robe was called the Chrisom, and if the child died within a month, it was shrouded in this robe, and was called a Chrisom-child. Parochial registers very frequently have the expression applied to children who are buried, and it will be remembered by readers of Shakespeare. Sometimes the cloth was called the Christening Palm. Later, say a hundred years ago, though the arraying by the minister was not in use, a newly baptized child was arrayed in a palm or pall to be brought down to see company.

In Perthshire, it is said, a child who was about to be privately baptized was placed in a clean basket covered over with a cloth, in which was placed a portion of bread and cheese. The basket was then hung on the iron crook over the fire, and turned round three times. It was to counteract the malignant spells of witches and evil spirits. Here is an inventory of christening garments of the seventeenth century (Notes and Queries):– 1. A lined, white figured satin cap.

2. A lined, white satin cap, embroidered with sprays in gold coloured silk.

3. A white satin palm, embroidered to match. Size 44 in. by 34 in.

4. A pair of deep cuffs, white satin, similarly embroidered, trimmed with lace, evidently intended to be worn by the bearer of the infant.

5. A pair of linen gloves or mittens for the baby, trimmed with narrow lace, the back of the fingers lined with coloured figured silk.

6. A palm, 54 in. by 48 in., of rich still yellow silk lined with white satin.

According to Sarum use, yellow was the altar colour for confessors festivals. This yellow pall may have been considered specially suitable at the childs being first openly pledged to confess the faith of Christ crucified. Another name for the. christening palm is the christening sheet or "cude cloth." This is a superstition that if it is not burned within a year of the childs birth it will never be able to keep a secret.

The gift of " Apostle Spoons " by sponsors is said, by Stow, to have originated in the days of Queen Elizabeth. Shakespeare, on being godfather to one of Ben Jonsons children, gave him "a dozen of Latten spoons." In the days of James I. it was the fashion for sponsors to give shirts with little bands or cuffs wrought with silk or blue thread, but this did not last, they went back to spoons or cups.

Brand quotes from " The Comforts of Wooing":–" The godmother hearing when the child was to be coated, brings it a gill coral, a silver spoon and porringer, and a brave new tankard of the same metal." According to Shipman the custom of making presents at baptisms declined in the time of the Commonwealth.

Pepys, however, observed the custom:–"Nov. 24th. At my goldsmiths, bought a basin for my wife, to give the parsons child, to which the other day she was godmother. It cost me;1o 14s. besides graving, which I do with the cyphers name, Daniel Mills."

Christening tongs were also a favourite present, which were of the same size as an ordinary pair of sugar tongs, but were in the form of a stork standing upright upon the claws which partly form the handle. When opened for the purpose of grasping the sugar, the body, which is hollow, discloses the image of a baby in swaddling clothes.

This no doubt originated in the old Teutonic fiction that newly-born babes were brought by storks.

Here are a few Scottish notes of gifts from the child to its parents. They are all from various columns of Notes and Queries:– In 1871, a gentleman was met in one of the principal streets of Edinburgh by a very respectably dressed female, with a nurse carrying a child. They stopped him, and the former presented him with a paper bag containing a biscuit, a bit of cheese, and a bit of gingerbread. On his expressing surprise, she said, "Oh! sir, it is the christening bit."

In country places in Scotland, it was a custom, now nearly exploded, for the mother on the way to baptism to take a supply of bread and cheese, a " whang " or slice of which she gave to the first person she met on the country road after leaving church, and it was accounted a high insult to refuse it. Probably the provision was part of the " blythe" meat presented to the friends in the house, who had assembled after the birth to offer congratulations. Such offerings may perhaps be traced to the period when the old Romans inhabited the Caledonian regions.

In 1855, at Candleriggs, a silver coin was given in return for the eatables. The appearance of copper was, if possible, to be avoided.

In Fifeshire, before starting for the kirk, the "christening-piece," consisting of shortbread, cheese, and oatcake, was made up into a white paper parcel tied with ribbon; this the mother held in her right hand as she left the house, and presented to the first person met by her, whether stranger or friend, gentle or simple. The "christening-piece" was always gladly accepted, and in return kind wishes were expressed for the future happiness of the child.

It is noticeable that at the other end of Great Britain we have the same idea.

At Looe, in Cornwall, the gift was generally a small cake made for the purpose, and called the "christening crib," crib being a provincialism for a bit of bread. At Polperro, three miles from Looe, a gift" termed the " kimbly " was also made to the person who brought the first news of a birth to those interested in the new arrival.

This custom was still practised in Devonshire in 1883.

Where children are brought in batches to be baptized, as is often the case in large towns, it is curious to note that superstitions exist about the precedence of sexes, though in different places the ideas are contrary. Thus in the North of England there are places where the parents are very anxious that the girls should be taken first, on the ground that otherwise the boys will be beardless. In Surrey and Worcestershire the same desire is expressed; in the West of Scotland the males have precedence. The old ideas can hardly be classed under superstitions. In those churches, where now-a-days ancient rules are revived, Holy Communion is always administered to men before women, and Confirmation to boys. Maskell, in his Monumenta Ritualia, Eccl., Angl., 1-23, quotes the following rubric from Bishop Leofrics missal:–" Et accipiat presbyter eos a parentibus eorum, et baptizantur primi masculi cleinde feminae, sub trina mersione, Sanctam Trinitatem. sernel invocando."

Cases are on record where a cottagers tenth child was christened with a sprig of myrtle in its cap to mark it as the tithe child; it is said that a Rector of Compton recognized such a tithe child, and sent him to school.

One of the silliest and most mischievous pieces of legislation was the Act 23, George III., c. 67. It enacted that after the 1st of-October, 1783, stamp duty of 3d. should be paid to His Majesty on the entry of every marriage, birth, or christening, in the register of every parish, precinct, or place in Great Britain, under penalty of,5 for each entry. And that the churchwardens should provide a book for each entry, and the parson, vicar, curate, and other person receiving the duty was to be allowed 2s. in the , for his trouble. By 25 George III., c. 75, the tax was extended to dissenters. People were furious, and the poor parson, who was supposed to be charging for his own benefit, got the hardest words. The Act was repealed by 34 George III., c. 11, the tax ceasing October 1st, 1794.

In conclusion, we will put together a few odds and ends of folk lore. In Ayrshire, in the end of the last century, when a child was taken to a distance to be baptized, a quantity of salt was placed round it before leaving the house, to ward off evil.

In Worcestershire, it is considered that if an engaged couple stand as god-parents to the same child, it is a sure sign that their engagement will never end in marriage. This is clearly a relic of what we have already noticed, the mediaeval church law by which those persons who stood in any spiritual relationship to one another were thereby debarred from contracting marriage.

In Dalston, Carlisle, there is a belief that if the baptism of a child takes place after it has been " shortened," the baby will not only be noisy and disagreeable in church during the administration of the sacrament, but will remain bad-tempered and ill-natured for ever afterwards.

The belief still prevails in many rural districts that children dying unbaptized wander in woods and solitudes lamenting their hard fate. In Sweden parents will, therefore, carry a child miles away in the depth of winter to the minister to have it baptized before it is half-a-day old. There are, however, methods by which it is supposed even if baptism be deferred, that the devils power over the child can be neutralized. One is to wrap it in red cloth and lay it in its cradle, with a psalm book and a pair of scissors placed crosswise upon its breast.

"In presenting a child to the minister, its head must be on the right arm of the male parent." (West of Scotland).

Brand quotes from a book on Scotland, published in 1793, the statement that the inhabitants of Kirkwall and S. Ola would consider it as an unhappy omen were they by any means disappointed in getting their children baptized on the very day which they had previously fixed in their minds for that purpose.

The same compiler has this:—In the North, when the child was taken to church to be christened, a little boy was engaged to meet the infant on leaving the house, because it was deemed an unlucky omen to encounter a female first.

It is supposed to be lucky for children to cry at baptisms, as if they are quiet and good then it shows they are too good to live. The idea arose from the custom of exorcism. When the devil was going out of a possessed person it cried and rent him sore; therefore the tears and struggles of the infant would be convincing proof that the evil one had departed. In Ireland, the nurses pinch the baby rather than let it be silent or cheerful.

In Scotland (to quote Brand once more), on their return from church, they take the newly baptized child and vibrate it three or four times gently over a flame, saying thrice, "Let the flame consume thee now or never." This is possibly derived from a feast called Amphidromia, held at Athens, by private families on the fifth day after the birth of the child, when it was the custom of the gossips to run round the fire with the infant in their arms, and then, having delivered it to the nurse, they were entertained with feasting and dancing.

Another Scotch fancy is that it is unlucky to tell the names of infants before baptism.

In one of Dekkers plays (1630) occurs the following:—I am the most wretched fellow, sure some left-handed priest christened tne, I am so unlucky.

In Greece, while the father is alive, none of his sons are baptized with his name; thus a father and son never have the same Christian name at the same time. But on the death of the father it is customary for one of his sons to adopt his name. The eldest son always bears the name of his paternal grandfather (a common custom in Scotland), even though the latter be alive. On the other hand, for the obvious reason of identification, an illegitimate son always takes the baptismal name of his father. It is probable that this practice arises from a belief that the father would die on giving to his son precisely his own name, and that the Greek church does not allow the variation of a second Christian name.

(tnstoma.

By England Howlett, F. s. a.

IN all ages, and in all countries, a halo of interest attaches to the marriage ceremony, and formerly, when superstition was so rife in the country, it naturally followed that all sorts of curious customs arose in connection with marriage–customs which, at the time of their inauguration, were full of meaning and real interest, but many of which in process of time, and owing to an altered state of society, have fallen either into oblivion, or become so changed as to be hardly recognisable.

Marriage, in one form or other, is the oldest institution of society, and the source of its most ancient laws. The primitive ceremonies of marriage are of immense number, and many of them have left distinct survivals in modern customs. As regards Christian Europe, in 1085 Hildebrand declared Marriage to be a sacrament of the Church; and, at the Reformation, Calvin declared it to be an institution of God. The School of Grotius, on the other hand, describes it as a contract of partnership.

The Anglo-Saxon marriage ritual was for the parties, with their attendants, to come to the porch of the Church: here they were met by the priest; first he blessed the ring and gave it to the bridegroom, who placed it on the middle finger of the brides left hand. After this the priest recited a form of blessing over the parties; then he led them into the Chancel where they remained while mass was celebrated, towards the close of which they received the solemn nuptial benediction, and afterwards the Pax, and the holy communion.

Before the Council of Trent a valid marriage in the eyes of the church might be effected by a simple declaration of the parties to be man and wife; no witnesses were necessary under these circumstances, and the presence of a priest might also be dispensed with. It will at once be seen that a practice such as this was open to very great and grave abuse where the interested parties were only too often the only witnesses of the declaration. After the Council of Trent, and in all countries where the discipline of Trent is received and promulgated, the presence of the parish priest is absolutely necessary to constitute a valid marriage in the eyes of the Roman Church by mere declaration of the parties to be man and wife, and under no circumstances can marriages such as these be recognized by the law.

It was customary in many places for the priest to entwine the ends of his stole round the joined hands of the bride and bridegroom, at the words "Those whom God hath joined together," in token of the indissoluble union thereby effected. Most probably this practice led to the familiar expression " Tying the knot." Neither the Roman nor the Sarum Missals contain any direction for this ritual, which would appear to be a pure innovation on the part of the priests.

In ancient Rome the Patrons or Patricians only might marry with each other. If a Patrician married a client or vassal, their children were not allowed to take Patrician rank; because these clients or vassals had not connubium, or right of marriage with their Patrons. Under Caesars rule a married woman was allowed the use of more ornaments, and more costly carriages, than the laws of Rome permitted to women generally. A married man who had three children born at Rome, or four born in Italy, or five in the provinces, enjoyed freedom from certain duties and charges: this no doubt was done to encourage the marriage tie, which at that time had become exceedingly lax.

The drinking of wine in the Church at weddings is enjoined by the Hereford Missal. The Sarum Missal directs that sops immersed in wine, as well as the liquor itself, and the cup containing it, should be blessed by the priest. The beverage was drunk not only by the bride and bridegroom, but by the rest of the company. A distinct survival of this custom, although in a debased form, lingered beyond the middle of the present century, at Whitburn, in Durham, where the custom of giving what they called Hot-Pots was kept up; that is, on the conclusion of the marriage service the bride and bridegroom were served in the porch with steaming compounds of brandy, ale, sugar, eggs, spices, etc., the bridesmaids also partook of this, and the remainder was distributed amongst the guests. The custom of nuptial drinking appears also to have prevailed in the Greek Church: and the Jews have a custom at the present day, when a couple are married, to break the glass in which the bride and bridegroom have drunk, to remind them of mortality.

The use of torches at weddings is very ancient.

At Rome the practice was that two children should lead the bride, and a third carry before her a torch of white thorn. The Greeks used also a nuptial torch, which was carried by the brides mother. Lamps and flambeaux are used at Japanese weddings, and torches are still used at Turkish marriages.

Knives formerly formed part of the accoutrements of a bride. This is easily accounted for by the fact that anciently it formed part of the dress for women to wear a knife sheathed and suspended from their girdles. A bride says to her jealous husband, in Dekkers Match me in London, 1631:

"See at my girdle hang my wedding knives!
With those despatch me."

The use of bridesmaids at weddings is of remote antiquity. Amongst the Anglo-Saxons the bride was led to the Church by a matron, who was called the brides woman, and followed by a company of young girls who were called bridesmaids. It was at one time the custom for the bridesmaids to lead the bridegroom to Church, and for the bridegrooms men to conduct the bride. This is clearly alluded to in the Colliers Wedding:

"Two lusty lads, well drest and strong,
Stepd out to lead the bride along:
And two young maids of equal size,
As soon the bridegrooms hands surprise."

The bridegrooms men were anciently called Bride Knights, which was an appropriate name at the period when they actually fulfilled that office.

Bride cake is of ancient origin: it is a relic of the Roman period, when the marriage ceremony consisted principally of the contracting parties partaking of a cake made of flour, salt, and water, in the presence of the Pontifex Maximus, or High Priest, and ten witnesses. The form of the cake has varied in different ages. Ben Jonson refers to it in the Tale of a Tub, iii., 8:

"The maids and her half-valentine have plyd her,
With courtise of the Bride cake and the bowl,
As she is laid awhile."

As feasting was connected with nearly all religious ceremonies, and as each feast speedily appropriated its particular article of food, the bride cake became inseparably associated with the bridal feast. Anciently, small cakes were made for weddings, and distributed amongst the guests; the ingredients of these doubtless changed from age to age, but there is little doubt the cake was always a sweet one which, in the early days, would be sweetened with honey with spices in it, and, after their introduction, currants. In the seventeenth century it was usual for the bride and bridegroom to kiss over the cake, and many are the superstitions connected with it.

It was formerly the custom for the brides to go to church with their hair hanging loose behind. Anne Boleyns was thus dishevelled when she went to the altar with Henry VIII. Webster refers to this practice in 7 he White Devil:
"And let them dangle loose as a brides hair."

Nuptial garlands or wreaths are of great antiquity; they were equally used by both the Jews and the Heathens. The Roman custom was for the bride to have a chaplet of flowers or herbs upon her head, whilst among the Anglo-Saxons, after the benediction in the church, both the bride and bridegroom were crowned with flowers. In the Eastern church the chaplets used at marriages were first blessed by the priest. Wreaths made of ears of corn were frequently worn by brides in the time of Henry VIII., and myrtle was also much used for this purpose. In many churches it was usual to keep a crown of metal for the use of brides, and for which they would pay a fee. In the churchwardens accounts of St. Margarets, Westminster, for the year 1540, is the following entry:–"Paid to Alice Lewis, a goldsmiths wife, of London, for a serclett to marry Maydens in, the 26th day of September,,3 Ids. od."

Marriage by proxy was probably practised by the heathen Romans, and even so late as the middle ages was not at all uncommon, although then it had become confined principally to the aristocracy, and later on few instances are to be met with, except in the case of Royalty. Henry VIII. married Anne of Cleves by proxy. So also James II., when Duke of York, in 1673, was married by proxy to Mary of Modena. The church always looked with great disfavour on this form of marriage, and for this reason the parties were generally re-married on the arrival of the bride in her husbands country, or at the home of the bridegroom.

Amongst the ancient Northern nations a knot appears to have been considered as the symbol of love, faith, and friendship, pointing out, as it were, the indissoluble tie of affection and duty; hence it is that knots or bows of ribbon came to be used as wedding favours, a particular form of which came to be known as the True Lovers Knot. The peasantry of France wore the bridal favour on the arm, whereas in England it was formerly worn in the hat, and consisted of ribbons of various colours; in later years white ribbon alone was used. Curiously enough Rosemary was not only carried at funerals, but was also worn at weddings, and appears to have been considered as an insignia of a wedding guest: on these occasions the sprigs of Rosemary were frequently gilded, or dipped in scented water. Bay leaves were also used for a similar purpose, but not so generally as the Rosemary.

Wedding rings were used both by the Greeks and Romans, but then only at the ceremony of betrothal, and not that of marriage. The Anglo-Saxon bridegroom at the betrothal gave a Wed, or pledge, and a ring was placed on the maidens right hand, where it remained until marriage, and was then transferred to the left. During the reigns of George I. and George II., the wedding ring was often worn on the thumb. The placing of the ring on the book is a remnant of the ancient custom of blessing the ring by sprinkling Holy Water in the form of a cross, and this is still done in the Roman Church. One of the earliest forms of rings was the Gemel, or double ring, and this was used as a pledge before marriage: they were generally made in three parts, and broken in the presence of a witness, who retained the third part. In Germany, Sweden, Norway, and Denmark, it was a common custom for the engaged couple each to give to the other a plain gold ring, much resembling a wedding ring. In the last century, wedding rings were frequently inscribed with poesys. Dr. John Thomas, who was Bishop of Lincoln in 1753, married four times. The motto or poesy on the wedding ring at his fourth marriage was:–

"If I survive
Ill make them five."

King Henry VIII. gave Anne of Cleves a ring with the poesy:–

"God send me well to keep."

It was a general custom in the middle age for the bridegroom to place the ring first on the thumb of the bride, then on her second finger, and then on her third, at the name of each person of the Trinity, " leaving ft " as the rubric directs, on her fourth finger at the word Amen; thus signifying by action, not less than by word, that he was undertaking the duties of the married state, " in the name of the Father, of the Son, and of the Holy Ghost." The reason assigned for the fourth finger being appointed as the final resting place of the wedding ring, is because on that finger there is generally believed to be a certain vein which proceeds to the heart. The left hand most probably was appointed because the virgins espoused to the church wore the ring of their celestial nuptials on the right hand.

See Edwards History and Poetry of Finger Rings, Cap. 5, p. 221.

The nuptial kiss was a solemn ceremony which was duly directed both by the Sarum and York Uses. At the " Sanctus," in the bridal mass, both the bride and the bridegroom knelt near the altar; if neither of them had been married before, a pall, or as it used to be called, the " care-cloth," was held over them at its four corners by as many clerics. After the " Pater Noster," and just before the " Pax," the priest turning himself towards the married couple gave them the nuptial blessing. The care-cloth was then removed, and the bridegroom arose from his knees and received the kiss of peace from the priest; he then turned to his bride and kissed her upon the cheek. In the York Use the care-cloth was held by only two clerics. Although the solemn ceremonial of the nuptial kiss has long since ceased to be a regular portion of the marriage service, still, in many rural districts, it is customary for the bridegroom to kiss the bride while they are before the altar, and in sight of the congregation assembled. At Halse, a village in Somersetshire, it is still a recognised custom amongst the labouring classes for the bridegroom, after he has placed the ring on the brides finger, to take her in his arms and kiss her fervently,-and it is a somewhat remarkable feature that instead of this causing any amusement amongst the spectators, it is treated as a solemnity, and would certainly appear to be a distinct survival of the nuptial kiss. A similar custom still prevails at Bishops Lydeard, in Somersetshire.

There is a rule in Hindoo law which forbids a younger sister to be married before the elder; nor is a younger brother allowed to be married before the elder. There would seem to be a curious resemblance between these rules and the rules of the Old Testament days, when Laban refused to let his younger daughter marry before Leah. We get another instance of a restraint on marriage, in 1367, when the memorable Parliament of Kilkenny was held, which passed the Statute of Kilkenny. By this statue it was declared high treason for any person of English origin to marry into an Irish family.

Poor maidens who might otherwise lose their chance of matrimony for want of a dowry were sometimes provided for by funeral doles. " I will," says Richard Trowler, A. d. 1477, "that X/. be disposed of at my burying among poor people, and that X/. be given to the marriage of poor maidens not having father or mother." Johanne Beauchamp, Lady of Bergavenny, devised " to the marriage of poer maydens dwellyng withyn my lordship, C/, and to the makyng and emending of febull brugges and foul weyes, C/." There certainly seems to be a curious analogy between this custom and the laws of ancient Greece, by which the State provided a dowry for those maidens who, through poverty or plainness, would otherwise have remained unmarried.

With regard to the seasons for celebrating marriage, the Church was formerly very strict. The parish register for St. Marys, Beverley, contains the following entry under date November-2 5, 1641:–

"When Advent comes do thou refraine,
Till Hillary set ye free again,
Next Septuagessima saith thee nay,
But when Low Sunday comes thou may,
Yet at Rogation thou must tarrie,
Till Trinitie shall bid thee marry.".

The above appears to have been a popular verse to inscribe in registers, for, with slight variations, it is to be met with in several parishes. Philomatrs Almanac, for the year 1674, contains similar rules in prose:–

" Times Prohibiting Marriage This Year.

Marriage comes in on the 13th of January, and at Septuagessima Sunday it is out again until Low Sunday, at which time it comes in again, and goes not out till Rogation Sunday. Then it is forbidden until Trinity Sunday, from whence it is unforbidden till Advent Sunday, but then it goes out, and comes not in again till the 13th of January next following."

With regard to the publication of Banns of Marriage, it appears to have been the custom in the primitive ages that the Church should be forewarned of marriages. The earliest existing canonical enactment on the subject in the English church, is that in the eleventh canon of the Synod of Westminster, in the year 1200, which enacts that "no marriage shall be contracted without banns thrice published in the church, unless by the special authority of the Bishop." Anciently, before the publication of banns, it was the custom for the curate to affiance the two persons to be married in the name of the Trinity; and at this period the banns were sometimes published at Vespers as well as at Mass.

Forbidding the banns of marriage is now a very rare occurrence; formerly, it was not so, and it was customary to interdict a marriage sometimes for the sole purpose of making a comparative stranger prove his bona-fides. The parish register of Frampton, near Boston, Lincolnshire, contains the following entry on January, 1, 1653:–The marriage of Edward Morton and Jane Goodwin was objected to by John Ayne, Thomas Appleby, and William Eldred: because in the first place, the said Edward Morton was a stranger, and they did not know where he had lived until a short time before, or whether he was married or single; therefore they desired the marriage might be deferred until he brought a certificate of these things. And secondly because they have been informed and do believe that he is a very poor man, and therefore they wish him to get some sufficient man to be bound with him to secure the town from any charge of him or his."

An interesting custom is still kept up at Laceby, a village in North Lincolnshire, where the bells ring a merry peal at the close of the service in which the third publication of banns has taken place. A similar custom prevailed at North Kelsey, in Lincolnshire, the practice there being to ring the peal of bells on the Monday evening after the last publication of banns, but in this latter case the custom appears to have fallen into disuse many years ago. Bells frequently bear inscriptions relating to the marriage peals; the fifth bell at Coton-in-the-Elms, Derbyshire, dated 1786, has inscribed on it:–

"The bride and groom we greet In holy wedlock joined,
Our sounds are emblems sweet
Of hearts in love combined."

In the early part of the century it appears to have been a common practice-in most parts of the country for the clerk, after the publication of the banns of marriage,, to rise and say, "God speed them well;" and in some places it was usual for the congregation to respond " Amen." At Hope, in Derbyshire, this was done not only on the publication of banns, but also at the solemnization of the marriage, immediately after the abjuration–" I require and charge you both." The practice has fallen into the same oblivion which has overtaken the old parish clerk–at one period so self-important an individual in the church, and now, except in remote villages, so insignificant an official. The custom appears to have lingered for some time at Croxton Kerrial, near Melton Mowbray, and at Birkby, a village near Northallerton.

The following extract from the parish registers for Chalgrave, Bedfordshire, for the year 1655, furnishes an instance of the manner in which weddings were frequently conducted during the Commonwealth, in pursuance of Cromwells Act of Parliament, August 24, 1653, and by which the presence of a priest was entirely dispensed with:–" Henry Fisher and Sarah Newson, of Chalgrave, published three severall Lords dayes in one psh meeting house called the church ended xxiij"1 of Septb and no exception made against it, and the said Henry Fisher and Sarah Newson was married the xxixth Septb, as by certificate doth appear by Francis Austeres Esq, and in psents of Will: Martin and Abraham Newson." In the parish registers of Launceston, Cornwall, is the following entry:–" Hereap follow marriages by laymen, according to the prophanes, and giddynes of the times without precedent or example in any Christian Kingdom or Commonwealth, from the birth of Christ unto this very year 1655.

"1655, The 28th daye of October were married by John Hicks, Gent, and Maior of this Town, John Heddon and Mary Harvey. Their banns being published in the Markett Place att Launceston three severall Markett dayes, viz., the IIth, the 18th, and the 25th of this instant October, without contradiction."

The following extract from the register of St. Marys Church, Bermondsey, 1604, instances a. curious custom of re-uniting husband and wife who had been long separated:–

"The form of a solemn vowe made betwixt a man and his wife, having been long absent, through which occasion the woman beinge married to another man, took her again as followeth:–

The Mans spcach. Elizabeth, my beloved wife, I am right sorie that I have so long absented myself from thee, whereby thou shouddest be occasioned to take another man to be thy husband. Therefore I do now vowe and promise in the sight of God, and this companie, to take thee again as mine owne, and will not only forgive thee, but also dwell with thee, and do all other duties unto thee, as I promised at our marriage.

The Womans speache. Raphe, my beloved husband, I am right sorie that I have in thy absence taken another man to be my husband: but here, before God, and this companie, I renounce and forsake him, and do promise to keep mysellfe only unto thee during life, and to perform all duties which I first promised unto thee in our marriage.

The first day of August, 1604, Raphe Goodchild of the parish of Barkinge, in Thames Street, and Elizabeth his wife, were agreed to live together, and thereupon gave their hands one to another, makinge either of them a solemn vowe so to do in the presence of us:

William Steve, Parson,

Edward Coker, and Richard Eives, Clerk."

In Germany a sect of the Moravians called Herrnhuters have a most curious method of selecting their life partners: the men and women of a marriageable age are collected in a house which has a suite of three rooms, each opening into the other, the young men in one end room and the young women in the other; then the doors from these two rooms are thrown open into the middle room, which is perfectly darkened. After this follows a sort of general scramble, or " catch who can," and whichever girl the man catches becomes his wife. This method of selecting a wife seems somewhat risky, but it is possible that even in a darkened room a couple with a prior attachment might manage to tumble into each others jarms, and so, while adhering in the letter to the custom of their sect, bring about the union dictated by their hearts.

The throwing of an old shoe after a newly-married couple on their departure is general all over the country, but in Kent the custom is accompanied by a little more detail than is usually observed in other parts of the country. The principal bridesmaid throws the shoe, the other bridesmaids run after it, the belief being that the one who gets it will be the first to be married. She then throws the shoe amongst the gentlemen, and it is supposed that the one who is hit will also be married before the others.

The custom of showering rice over the bride and bridegroom is a universal one, although in some parts wheat is substituted, this was formerly general in Nottinghamshire and Sussex. The practice appears to find a parallel in Poland, when, after the nuptial benediction has been given by the priest, the father receives the newly-married couple at the door of their house, and strews some barley corns over their heads. These corns are carefully gathered up and sown. If they grow it is considered an omen that the married pair will enjoy a life of happiness. Grain of any sort is symbolical of plenty, and no doubt at different periods and in different countries that grain has been selected which could be" procured the most easily. An old Spanish ballad of the sixteenth century, The Cids Wedding, refers to the custom, except that ears of wheat appear to have been used instead of threshed wheat:–

"All down the street the ears of wheat are round
Ximena flying."

Wedding Biddings were usual down to the end of the last century: these were entertainments given previously to the wedding, and the guests were each expected to bring a present. An account of these presents was preserved, and it was expected that the giver should receive a gift of equal value on their own marriage. In Cumberland, at these entertainments, a bowl or plate was fixed in some convenient part of the house where each of the company contributed in money in proportion to his ability or inclination. In some districts the bidding was publicly done by a herald with a crook or wand adorned with ribbons, who gave a general invitation according to a prescribed form.

Gretna Green was the invariable resort of runaway couples, owing to the flaw in the Old Scottish law which required nothing more than an acknowledgment before witnesses in order to constitute a valid marriage. The Marriage Act of 1856 has, however, rendered such unions impossible, for by its provisions, which are common to both countries, it is necessary that one of the parties shall have resided for at least twenty-one days in the parish where the marriage takes place. The old romantic interest once attached to Gretna Green is now fast becoming a thing of the past.

The following extract from the register of St. Martins Parish, Leicester, is interesting as showing how, in the time of Queen Elizabeth, a marriage was celebrated in a case where a bridegroom was deaf and dumb.

"Decimo quinto Februarii. 18. Eliz.: reginae.
Thomas Filsby and Ursula Russet were married; and
because the said Thomas is naturally deaf and dumb,
could not for his part observe the order of the form of marriage, after the approbation had of Thomas, the Bishop of Lincoln, John Chippendale, LL. D., and Commissary, and Mr. Richard Davis, of Leicester, and. others of his brethren, with the rest of the parish, the said Thomas for expressing of his mind instead of words, of his own accord used these signs: First he embraced her with his arms, took her by the hand, and put a ring on her finger, and laid his hand upon his heart and held up his hands towards heaven; and to show his countenance to dwell with her till his lifes end, he did, by closing his eyes with his hands, and digging the earth with his feet, and pulling as though he would ring a bell, with other signs approved."

An interesting feature in the marriage announcements a century ago, was the detail given respecting the fortune of the bride. Matters which now we regard as more or less private were then openly advertised to the world. Williamsons Liverpool

Advertiser for 1759, contains the following notice: " Liverpool, May 25. On Tuesday last was married at Hale, Dr. Zachariah Leafe, of Prescot, to Miss Martha Clough, of Halewood, an agreeable young lady of 18 years of age, with a very genteel fortune." The Leeds Intelligencer, for July 3, 1764, announces:–"On Thursday last was married Mr. John Wormald, of this town, merchant, to Miss Rebecca Thompson, daughter of the late–Thompson, Esqr., of Staincliffe Hall, near Batley, an agreeable young lady with a fortune of upwards of.4,000." These are no uncommon instances, and almost any newspaper of the period would furnish similar examples.

It was a common custom, down to about 1850, for butchers boys, in their blue coats, and sometimes also with a large white favour, to attend in the front of houses where weddings had that day taken place, and play on their cleavers with knuckle bones; the " Butchers Serenade" it was called. Hogarth, in his delineation of the marriage of the industrious apprentice to his masters daughter, introduces a set of butchers coming forward with marrow bones and cleavers.

A bridegroom was often called upon to pay toll. It was a Somersetshire custom for the village children, on the occasion of a wedding, to fasten the churchyard gates with a wreath of evergreens and flowers; a floral bond which always required a " Silver Key " to unlose. A writer to Notes and Queries, in January, 1858, states that on the occasion of his marriage, some years previously, when passing through the village adjoining that in which the marriage had taken place, his carriage was stopped by the villagers, holding a band of twisted evergreens and flowers, who good naturedly refused to let the carriage pass until toll had been paid.

At Burnley, in Lancashire, an old custom prevailed by which all persons married at St. Peters Church, in that town, paid a fine to the boys at the Grammar School; the money thus obtained being applied, according to the records, for the maintenance of the school library. This custom appears to have been kept up down to the year 1870, about which time Burnley Grammar School was rebuilt, and, on its re-opening, the practice of paying fines to the boys was discontinued.

It is a common saying in Lancashire that a bride should wear at her wedding:–

"Something old and something new,
Something borrowed, something blue."

This saying, and the practice of it, is common in other parts of England; the writer knows a lady who, when married at Bedford, five years ago, carried out the couplet to the letter; on this same bride being brought by her husband to his home in Lincolnshire, at the end of the honeymoon, the custom of lifting the bride over the threshold was observed; the bride and bridegroom got out of the carriage a few yards from the house, and he carried her up the steps, and into the hall. This was formerly a common practice in the North of England, and in Scotland, and is the remains of an old Roman custom which has survived the onslaught of time and change.

It was an old custom to strew the path from the house of the bride to the church with sawdust or sand, and so recently as the year 1876 a "sawdust wedding " took place from a house in Sunderland. The custom would originate, no doubt, in a desire to secure a clean path for the bride to walk upon, and this was often ornamented with devices, which would be easily done with either material.

"Keeping the doorstep warm " was a custom practised most commonly in the North of England. As soon as the bride and bridegroom had gone away, and the old shoe had been thrown, a servant, or sometimes the guests, would pour a kettle of boiling water over the front doorstep, as an auspice that there would soon be another wedding from the same house–keeping the threshold warm for another bride they called it.

In these prosaic nineteenth century days, there is not much attention paid to the selection of the day of the week for the marriage ceremony. Our ancestors had many proverbs and couplets, all more or less pointing to certain and the same day, to avoid or select for the event.

Monday for wealth,
Tuesday for health,
Wednesday best day of all,
Thursday for losses,
Friday for crosses,
Saturday no luck at all.

The practice of inserting wedding announcements in newspapers is almost universal, and the addition of " no cards" appears as often as not. Our neighbours on the other side of the Atlantic have, however, quite outdone us by the following addition to a wedding announcement in the Quebec Morning Chronicle, of November 7th, 1868:–" No cards. No Cake. No Wine."

Burial Customs.

By England Howlett, F. s. a.

THE burial of the dead furnishes many instances of curious customs, some of which, with modifications, survive to our own day, while a large number have become entirely obsolete, or meaningless. In the middle ages especially, it naturally followed that a great deal of superstition should be attached to death and burial, and superstition often originated a custom which survived long after any importance was attached to the origin.

The Egyptians made futile attempts to preserve the body by embalming–this practice originated no doubt in the opinion which it was said they held, that so long as a body remained uncorrupted, so long the soul continued in it. The Greeks usually, but not universally, burnt their dead, and interred their ashes in urns. The actual origin of cremation is lost in obscurity, most probably the primary idea was the purification of the body by fire. It is supposed the early practice of the Romans was to bury, but their later practice was to burn, and cremation was held by them in honour, the bodies of suicides and young children not being allowed to be burnt.

In ancient times burial was always without the walls of the cities and towns; indeed before the time of Christianity it was not lawful to bury the dead within the cities, but they used to be carried out into the fields, and there deposited. About the end of the sixth century, St. Augustine obtained of King Ethelbert a Temple of Idols (used by the King before his conversion), and made a burying place of it; and Saint Cuthbert afterwards obtained (a. d. 752) leave from the Pope to have yards made to the churches, suitable for the burial of the dead.

In the ordinary funerals of Christian Anglo-Saxons, the corpse was simply wrapped in linen, and carried to the grave by two persons, one holding the head, and the other the feet; the priest then censed the body, and whilst it was being deposited in the grave, offered up prayers and benedictions. At the obsequies of persons of distinction, hymns were sung by the attendant priests, who accompanied the body in procession. At this period the body of a deceased person was always watched by the relatives and friends from the moment of death to the time of burial; the " wake " of the present day being the survival of this custom.

It was a common practice, when the body was embalmed, to take out the heart and bowels, and inter them in a different church to that in which the body was buried; testators sometimes made a request in their wills for this to be done. The custom appears to have prevailed from the twelfth to the eighteenth century. The heart of Richard the First was buried at Rouen, his bowels at Chaluz, and his body at Fontevand. In 1838, the Kings heart was discovered under the pavement of the sanctuary in Rouen Cathedral, enclosed in a leaden case, with the inscription:–

Richard Cceur de Lion.
Due de Normandie. Roi DAngleterre.

Coeval with the introduction of church bells has been the appropriation of one of them to the service of the dying; originally this bell was tolled when one was yielding up life in order that all who heard it might offer up prayer for the departing spirit, and after death another bell was rung, called the " soul bell." The " Passing Bell," as it is now most inappropriately called, is not rung until some hours after death, and corresponds more nearly to the original" soul bell." In some districts it is always rung exactly twenty-four hours after death, the tenor bell being used for an adult, and the treble for a child; the big bell is generally reserved for funerals. In rural districts after the "passing bell" has tolled, the sex of the deceased is indicated most generally by tolling twice for a woman and thrice for a man, to this is often added the age by giving one toll for each year.

In the middle ages it was customary at the funeral of any great person to have his horse led, and armour borne, before his corpse, the horse being afterwards claimed as a mortuary due to the church at which the burial took place; the armour was either reserved for the next of kin of the deceased, or else was hung up in the church. No doubt much of the armour suspended over tombs is mere " undertakers trappings," although often considered genuine and of antiquity.

Over the tombs of bishops, the Episcopal mitre and pastoral staff was sometimes suspended, as in the case of those in Winchester Cathedral hanging over the tomb of Bishop Morley, who died in 1696; and of those in Bromsgrove Church, Worcestershire, suspended over the Monument of Dr. Hall, Bishop of Bristol, who died in 1710.

The hearse, so often mentioned in wills and funeral directions, was not a carriage for the conveyance of the body like that in use at the present day, but was a four square framework of timber, from each corner of which rose a rafter slanting, and all four rafters met at the top; this was covered with black cloth, and at the funerals of persons of distinction was set up for a time in the choir, for the reception of the body during the service; it was surrounded with rails, and fringed and. ornamented according to the rank of the deceased. Until the Reformation, hearses were garnished with numerous lights as well as with pencils and escocheons, but with the change of faith the lights were discontinued. These hearses were introduced about the fourteenth century, and they continued to be used until the civil wars of the seventeenth century.

In Shropshire there is a custom of "ringing the dead home," viz.: chiming all the bells, instead of ringing only one, while the funeral is on its way to the church. When the procession nears the churchyard gate the chiming is stopped and a minute bell is tolled. The sextons fees at Much Wenlock, as laid down in 1789, include "a chime if required before the funeral, o 1 o." At Hatherleigh, a small town in Devonshire, it was the prevalent custom to ring a lively peal on the church bells after a funeral, as elsewhere after a wedding-.

Even in the present day, in some remote rural districts, and especially in Hampshire, the practice still prevails of leaving open the outer door of the house, through which the corpse has been carried, until the mourners return from church, and in some places the custom extends also to the windows; this arises from a superstition that if the doors or windows be shut there will certainly be another death in the house within a year. In some districts there is a belief that if, when the moment of death approaches, all the doors and windows of the house are opened, the spirit will leave the body more easily.

It was an ancient practice to put an hour glass into the coffin before burial, as an emblem of the sand of life being run out. Some antiquaries are of opinion that little hour glasses were anciently given at funerals, like rosemary, and by the friends of the deceased either put into the coffin or thrown into the grave.

The custom which still prevails of sewing up a corpse in flannel, originated, doubtless, in the Act of Parliament, 18 and 19, Charles II., which was passed for the encouragement of the woollen trade, and required all bodies to be buried in woollen shrouds; two amending statutes were passed, 1678 and 1680, requiring at the funeral an affidavit to be delivered to the priest stating that the requirements of the law had been carried out; otherwise penalties were incurred. These acts were repealed by 54 George III., although long before that time the penalties for non-compliance with the law had ceased to be enforced. During the operation of the acts for burying in woollen, the law was sometimes evaded by covering the corpse with hay, or flowers, notification of which is sometimes met with in the parish registers.

Burial in armour was not at all uncommon in the middle ages, and was considered a most honourable form, of burial. Sir Walter Scott, in "The Lay of the last Minstrel," thus refers to it:

"Seemd all on fire that Chapel proud,
Where Roslins Chiefs uncoffind lie,
Each Baron for a sable shroud
Sheathed in his iron panoply."

Clement Spelman, of Narburgh, Recorder of Nottingham, who died in 1679, is immured upright, enclosed in a pillar in Narburgh Church, so that the inscription is directly against his face: this must surely be a solitary instance of burial in a pillar, although there are many other instances of burial in an upright position. Thomas Cooke, who was a Governor of the Bank of England, from 1737 to 1739, and who had formerly been a merchant residing in Constantinople, died at Stoke Newington, I2th August, 1752, and by his directions his body was carried to Morden College, Blackheath, of which he was a trustee, it was taken out of the coffin, and buried in a winding sheet upright in the ground, according to the Eastern custom. Ben Jonson was buried at Westminster in an upright position: possibly this may have been on account of the large fee demanded for a full-sized grave. It was for a long time supposed that the story was invented to account for the smallness of the gravestone, but on the grave being opened some years since, the dramatists remains were discovered in the attitude indicated by tradition. The following quotation from Hearnes "Collection of Anti quarian Discourses," Vol. I., p. 212, shows that the upright position of burial was anciently adopted in the case of captains in the army:

See Robinsons " History and Antiquities of Stoke Newington."

"For them above the grounde buryed, I have by tradition heard, that when anye notable Captayne dyed in battle or campe, the souldyers used to take his bodye and to sette him on his feet uprighte, and put his launce or pike into his hand, and then his fellowe souldyers did travell and everye man bringe so much earthe, and laye about him as should cover him, and mount up to cover the top of his pike."

At Messina there is a church attached to one of the monasteries–St. Jacomo–in which several monks are buried in a sitting posture, and may be seen through a grating in a vault below the church.

From the earliest ages to within about one hundred years ago, it appears to have been customary to bury either with or without a coffin. The following is an extract from a Terrier of lands, fees, etc., belonging to Caistor Vicarage, Lincolnshire, dated 1717: "For every grave in the churchyard and without coffin, four pence, if with coffin, one shilling." Amongst the Vestry Minutes of St. Helens, Bishopsgate, dated 5th March, 1564: "Item, that none shall be buryd within the Church, unless the dead corpse be coffined in wood." The late John Bernard Palmer, first Abbot of the Cistercians in England since the Reformation, was buried in the Chapter House, at Loughborough, without a coffin. In the days when burial without a coffin was general, the body was shrouded, tied at the head and feet, and carried to the grave in a closed bier, which was generally provided by the parish for this purpose.

A singular custom was wont to prevail at Gainsborough, of distributing penny loaves on the occasion of a funeral, to whosoever might demand them. Prior to the Reformation it was a common practice for our ancestors to direct in their wills that doles of bread and other alms should be given to the poor at their funerals; by this they performed a double act–relieving the corporal wants of the poor, and securing their prayers for the repose of their own souls. In some parts of Yorkshire, and elsewhere, it is still customary to send to friends immediately after death a paper bag of biscuits, and a card with the name, etc., of the deceased; this would not appear to be connected with a dole to purchase prayers, and may possibly find an origin in, and be the last remains of, the ancient ceremonial of the pagan burial feasts. At Amersden, in Oxfordshire, it was the custom at the burial of every corpse for a cake and flagon of ale to be given to the minister in the church porch immediately after the funeral.

The curious and repulsive practice of sin eating is now obsolete. Aubrey, in " Remains of Gentilisme and Judaisme," thus refers to it:–

"In the County of Hereford was an old custome at funeralls to have poor people who were to take upon them the sinnes of the party deceased. The manner was that when the corps was brought out of the house and layd on the Biere, a Loafe of Bread was brought out, and delivered to the Sinne eater over the corps, so also a Mazer-bowle of Maple full of beer, wch he was to drinke up, and six pence in money, in consideration whereof he took upon him all the sinnes of the Defunct, and freed him (or her) from walking after they were dead."

The origin of this strange custom was most likely connected in some way with the ceremony of the Scape Goat under the old Law. (Leviticus, cap. xvi., v. 21).

Tradition authorises the expectation that our Lord will appear in the east; therefore all the faithful dead are buried with their feet towards the east to meet Him. Hence in Wales the east wind is called "The wind of the dead mens feet." The eastern portion of a church yard is always looked on as the most honoured–next the south–then the west, and last of all the north, from the belief that in this order the dead will rise. A curious instance of this belief is furnished by an epitaph on a tombstone, dated 1807, on the north side of Epworth Churchyard, Lincolnshire, the last two lines of which run as follow:–

"And that I might longer undisturbed abide
I choosed to be laid on this Northern side."

Felons, and notorious bad characters, were frequently buried on the north side of the church.

In Suffolk most of the churches have both a north and south door, and, where old customs are observed, the body is brought in at the south door, put down at the west end of the aisle, and carried out by the north door. In Lincolnshire the north is generally reserved entirely for funerals, the south and west doors being reserved for christenings and weddings.

The burning of lights and torches at funerals has always been a mark of honour to the dead, and to have a great number was a special mark of honour to the deceased. Testators frequently made provision in their wills for the burning of torches, both as to the number to be used, and their price; these torches were generally provided by the churchwardens, and consequently they were an article of profit to the church. Churchwardens accounts furnish numerous instances of the charge to the friends of the deceased according to the consumption of wax.

The following extract from the will of John Woodford, of Barsby, in the parish of Ashby Folville, Leicestershire, dated 13th February, 1543, instances the custom of making minute testamentary arrangements for burial:–

"And my bodie to be burryed within the parishe Churche of our Ladie in Ashbie-folwcll Aforesaid as neare to the grave or Tombe of my cozin John Woodforde as maye be convenyentlie thought, or els in the crosse oyle before the pulpitt. Also I bequeath to our Mother Church of Lyncolne iiij1-Also to the Highe Altar xijd-Also I will that there be provided of Waxe xiij Tapers of the price of ij1l-a peece. Also I will that fyve poor men of the same parishe be chosen to beare fyve Torches about my hearse Att my burryall. And they doing shall have for their labour ijd-a peece. Also I bequeath to the same Church those fyve Torches And they to be burned att principal! Feasts and other Feasts as shall be convenyent. Also I will that every priest that cometh to my Burriall to have iiijd-and their dynner. And if there be no dynner, Then every priest tor to haveviijd-a peece. And the same priests of their charritie for to say dirge and Masse Alt my burriall or els Att home within their parish for my soule and for all my good Frends soules and for all xyen soules. Also I will that they shall ring att my Burriall and to have for their labour ijd-a peece."

The Arvel Dinner appears to be an ancient custom. This was properly a solemn festival on the day of interment, and when the corpse was exposed to view. The relations and friends were invited to attend so that, having inspected the body, they might avouch that the death was a natural one, and thus exculpate the heir and all others entitled to the deceaseds possessions from accusations of having used violence.

In Scotland the custom still prevails of taking down the window blinds at the death, and hanging white sheets across the windows. The custom also prevails in the north of England, and in many families a special sheet reserved for the death chamber is kept for the purpose, and often used from generation to generation.

In many parts of Scotland, too, it is still customary for the nearest relatives of the deceased to lower the body into the grave, and wait by the side until the grave is filled up.

In country districts in Wales a custom still exists of setting up a chest in the middle of the chance at the time of a funeral, and before leaving the church the mourners all file round and put their offerings in; this is really intended for the clergymans fee, but if the people are poor he often returns part of it (to a widow, for instance).

There is at least one instance that it was customary for the parish to provide an umbrella for the use of the clergyman on public occasions, more especially at funerals. The parish accounts at St. Johns, Chester, contain the following entries:– 1729 Paid Mr. George Marsh for an

Umbrell for the parish use—oo 10 6-1786 Paid for an Umbrell for Mr.

Richardson to read the Burial service under I 6 o- It was a general belief that if a corpse was carried over fields on the way to burial, it established a public right of way for ever, hence it became customary, when, for convenience, or in some cases out of necessity, a corpse was taken across fields, or over any private ground, for the undertaker to stick a number of pins in each gate as the procession went through. The pins were accepted by the owner of the land as a payment for the privilege of the corpse being carried through, and acted as an acknowledgment that the right of way was granted only for the particular occasion.

There is an ancient custom amongst the Russians to give the deceased two written documents placed in his coffin, containing (1) The confession of his sins: (2) The absolution given by the priest.

One of the ancient customs connected with Swedish funerals was to place a small looking-glass in the coffin of an unmarried female, so that when the last trump sounds she might be able to arrange her tresses. It was the practice for Scandinavian maidens to wear their hair flowing loosely, while the matrons wore it bound about the head, and generally covered with some form of cap, hence the unmarried woman was imagined as wakening at the judgment day with more untidy locks than her wedded sisters, and more in need of a glass.

It was customary, in carrying a corpse to burial, to rest the bier at any cross which might be in the way, whilst prayer was offered up; and, indeed, it was very general to erect a cross at any spot where the bier of a celebrated person had been rested on its way to interment.

In the fifteenth century a most revolting custom originated of representing on tombs a skeleton, or worse still, a corpse in a state of corruption; this was followed by the more becoming custom of representing the effigies of corpses enveloped in shrouds tied at the head and feet.

At Skipton it was an invariable practice to bury at midnight a woman who had died at the birth of her first child; the coffin was carried under a white sheet, the corners of which were held by four women. A custom prevailed in Lancashire when a mother died within a month of the birth of her child, of taking the baby to the funeral, and holding it over the grave as though to look in.

Towards the end of the fourteenth century arose the practice of carrying a waxen effigy of the deceased either on or before the coffin in the funeral procession. The earliest instance of this practice is in the case of King Henry V., whose effigy formed the first of those figures which are still preserved in Westminster Abbey. This custom was only observed in the case" of royalty, and persons of high position; the expense of a waxen representation of the deceased would prevent poor people from following it. The wax effigy of Oliver Cromwell lay in state while the body itselt was being embalmed, so that most probably the actual corpse was never exposed to public view. The practice appears to have been discontinued shortly after the Restoration.

A custom prevailed and continued even down to recent years of making funeral garlands on the death of young unmarried women of unblemished character. These garlands were made sometimes of metal, and sometimes of natural flowers or ever-greens, and commonly having a white glove in the centre, on which was inscribed the name, or initials, and age of the deceased. This garland was laid on or carried before the coffin during its passage to the grave, and afterwards frequently hung up in the church, generally being suspended from the roof. It was usual in the primitive church to place crowns of flowers on the heads of deceased virgins.

There was an order in the Church of England up to the year 1552, that if a child died within a month of baptism he should be buried in his chrisom in lieu o a shroud. The chrisom was a white baptismal robe with which, in mediaeval times, a child, when christened, was enveloped. A sixteenth century brass in Chesham Bois Church, in Buckinghamshire, represents Benedict Lee, chrisom child, in his chrisom cloth. The inscription underneath the figure stands thus:–

Of Rogr Lee gentilma, here lyeth the son Benedict Lee
Crysom who5 soule ihu pdo.

Formerly it was a general custom to erect crosses at the junction of four cross roads, on a place self-consecrated according to the piety of the age; suicides, and notorious bad characters, were frequently buried near to these, not with the notion of indignity, but in a spirit of charity, that, being excluded from holy rites, they, by being buried at cross roads, might be in places next in sanctity to ground actually consecrated.

The practice of placing a pewter plate containing a little salt on a corpse may possibly have originated in salt being considered an emblem of eternity. In Scotland the custom has generally been to place both salt and earth separate, and unmixed–the earth being an emblem of the corruptible body, and the salt an emblem of the immortal spirit. Salt has also been used to preserve a corpse. The body of Henry I., who died in Normandy, was cut and gashed, sprinkled with salt, wrapped in a bulls hide, and brought to Reading Abbey to be buried.

Testators frequently bequeathed palls by their wills for the general use of the parish; the following is an extract from the will of William Parkyns of Brympton, Berkshire, who died in 1558:–" Item, I will that mine executours buye one new pall, price 13s. 4d., the which I give unto the parish churche at Brympton to be laide uppon any personne, or personnes, that shall die within the said parishe and be brought to the churche."

In several rural districts in England, especially in the north, when a funeral takes place, a basin full of sprigs of box is placed at the door of the house where the corpse lies, and each person who attends the funeral takes a sprig of box as he enters the house, carries it in the funeral procession, and finally throws it into the grave of the deceased.

At Exford, near Minehead, it was formerly the custom for burials always to take place on a Sunday when possible, the burial service being dovetailed into the usual afternoon service. The corpse being brought into the church, was placed in front of the reading desk, and remained there during the service: the funeral psalms were read instead of the psalms for the day, and the funeral lesson instead of the second lesson. The burial service was concluded after the sermon, and the entire congregation would generally remain to the end. The custom appears to have fallen into disuse about thirty years ago.

Funeral cake or biscuit appears to be general in all parts. In Whitby, a round, flat, and rather sweet, sort of cake biscuit is baked expressly for use at funerals, and made to order by more than one baker in the town; it is white, slightly sprinkled with sugar, and of a fine even texture within. In Lincolnshire sponge finger biscuits are used. In Cumberland a custom prevailed of giving to each person who attended the funeral a small piece of rich cake, carefully wrapped up in white paper and sealed. This used to be carried round immediately before the "lifting of the corpse." Each visitor selected one of the sealed packets and carried it home unopened.

Funeral Bidders are most probably derived from the Romans, who used to send a public crier about inviting people to the solemnization of a funeral. In the northern countries each village had its regular " Bidder," who when " bidding" to the funeral generally knocked on the door with a key. In towns the crier frequently did the " bidding," having first called the attention of the people by his bell.

Concerning tbe

By John Nicholson.

IN the life of St. Willebald we are told " that it was an ancient custom of the Saxon nation on the estates of some of their nobles and great men, to erect, not a church, but the sign of the Holy Cross, dedicated to God, beautifully and honourably adorned, and exalted on high for the common use of daily prayer." It is the exception rather than the rule, for Domesday Book to mention a church in connection with a village, and it is possible that our Kirkbys, and place names having Kirk as a prefix, acquired that addition when the church was built in the churchyard ready for it–a churchyard already consecrated and hallowed by years of divine service and sacred memories.

What better place than this, in the whole township, could be found for the hearing of disputes and the settling of cases; here, where the bishop sat with the sheriff, where the clerics were lawyers, where oaths could be taken on everything that was holy, and round which all a mans sacred associations clustered. The churchyard was a court of justice; but in later times, the ecclesiastical authorities discouraged the holding of secular pleas in churches and churchyards. In 1287 a synod held at Exeter, said " Let not secular pleas be held in churchyards," but as late as 1472, a presentment from the parish of " Helemsay et Staunforthbrig" (Helmsley and Stamfordbrig) shews " that all the parishioners there hold pleas and other temporal meetings in the church and churchyard."

Acta SS. Ord. Benedict, sec. iii., part 2.

The great church festivals were much abused by traders. At these great gatherings, dealers in all kinds of goods appeared on the scene, spread their wares on the tombstones, and could with difficulty be kept out of the sacred edifice itself. Their noisy shoutings, the assemblage of pleasure seekers, and the tumult attending such gatherings interfered seriously with the Divine service proceeding inside the church. A presentment, in 1416, from St. Michael-le-Belfry, in the city of York, states " the parishioners say that a common market of vendibles is held in the churchyard on Sundays and holidays, and divers things, and goods, and rushes, are exposed there for sale, and horses stand over the bodies of the dead there buried, and defile the graves, to the great dishonour and manifest hindrance of divine worship, on account of the clamour of those who stand about." (Ibid., p. 248.) While so late as 1519, the churchwardens of Riccall, in Yorkshire, complain that "pedlars come on festival days into the porch of the church and there sell their merchandise." (Ibid., p. 271.)

York Fabric Rolls, p. 256.

Annual fairs were sometimes held in churchyards, especially where there was some saintly shrine or relic, which attracted crowds for the period of some anniversary. Perhaps Thomas-a-Becketts shrine at Canterbury was the most celebrated, but the shrine of Our Lady of Walsingham almost surpassed it. The common people held the idea that the Milky Way pointed towards Walsingham, and they called it Walsingham Way accordingly; while Glastonbury was called a second Rome for the number and sacredness of its relics. When the pilgrims had paid their devotion to the relics, they needed to eat and drink, and they were not averse to spend the rest of the day in amusement. Accordingly, minstrels, players, jugglers, and the like, supplied that demand, and the pilgrimage became a fair.

On Sundays and holidays, the churchyard became a public playground. In pre-Reformation days, a holiday was a holy-day, when man went not forth to his labour. Then there were no eight hours day, no Early Closing Associations, but work, work, work, from early morn till late night, the only cessation of toil being on Sundays and Saints days, hence termed a holy-day. On that day, people went to matins and mass in the morning, and spent the rest of the day in amusements, not always elevating or refined. The Synod of Exeter, already quoted, says, "We strictly enjoin on parish priests that they publicly proclaim in their churches, that no one presume to carry on combats, dances, or other improper sports in the churchyards, especially on the eves of the feasts of saints; or stage plays or farces, by which the honour of the churches is denied and sacred ordinances despised." Again, at Salton, Yorkshire, in 1472, " it is ordered, by the consent of the parishioners, that no one use improper and prohibited sports within the churchyard, as, for example, wrestling, football, and handball, under penalty of twopence forfeit." The ordinance seems to have been disregarded, or to have had only a temporary effect, for in 1519, a second complaint is made (Ibid., p. 270), when the ecclesiastica authorities commanded, "Let them desist on pain of excommunication."

In days when men went about armed with sword and dagger, it was sure to happen that a hasty quarrel would lead to stroke of sword or stab of dagger, without heed to the sacred character of the place, or to the fact that the assault constituted sacrilege, and desecrated "Gods Acre" by bloodshed.

Whitsuntide used to have a special feast of its own, known as Whitsun Ales or Church Ales, an institution by which money was obtained for repairing the church, helping the poor, and various charitable purposes. The churchwardens brewed the ale, and on the appointed day half the countryside assembled to join in the festivities;– music and song, baiting of bulls, bears, and badgers, bowls and ball, dice and card-playing, dancing and merry-making. The Church Ales were very popular in the North of England, where it was the practice to hold them in tents and booths erected in the churchyards. In 1651, in Somerset, seventy-two clergymen of the county certified that during these Church Ales, which generally fell on a Sunday, " the service of God was more solemnly performed, and the service better attended, than on other days."

York Fabric Rolls, p. 255.

As an instance of what could be accomplished at one of these Church Ales, we may mention that "in 1532, the little village of Chaddesden spent 34s. lod. on an Aell for the benefit of the great tower of All Saints, Derby, which was then being built, and earned by it,25 8s. 6d.,–near.400 of our money." (Lichfield, Diocesan Hist., S. p. c. k.)

Doles are often distributed in the churchyard. William Robinson, at one time Sheriff of Hull, when he died in 1708, left money to purchase a dozen loaves of bread, costing a shilling each, to. be given to twelve poor widows at his grave every Christmas Day. Leonard Dare, in 1611, directed that on Christmas Day, Lady Day, and Michaelmas Day, the churchwardens were "to buy, bring and lay on his tombstone, threescore penny loaves of good wholesome bread," which were to be distributed to the poor of the parish. A quaint custom is still enacted annually in London on

Good Friday. The vicar of St. Bartholomews the Great, Smithfield, drops twenty-one sixpences in a row on a certain ladys grave. The money is picked up by the same number of widows kneeling, who have previously attended service at the church, where a sermon is preached.

A quaint old custom, once not infrequently practised, was that of scrambling bread and cheese and other edibles in the churchyard. A story is told of two poor sisters walking to London to claim an estate. Arriving at Paddington, weary, hungry, and footsore, their miserable condition aroused sympathy, and the good folk of Padding-ton gave them relief. In course of time, their claim was established, and as a token of gratitude they left a bequest of bread and cheese, to be thrown from the top of the church of St. Marys, Paddington, among the people assembled in the churchyard below. This custom was continued into this present century, for in 1821, it is noticed in the newspapers as an annual practice to throw bread and cheese from the belfry of the church at eight oclock on the Sunday before Christmas Day. At Barford, Oxfordshire, is a piece of land, known as White-bread Close, the rent of which was formerly spent in buying bread to be scrambled for at the church door. A correspondent of the Gentleman s Magazine for 1824, says that the " distribution occasioned such scenes of indecent riot and outrage, even fighting in the church itself, that a late curate very properly effected the suppression of a practice productive of this gross abuse." Mr. Tuke, of Wath, near Rotherham, who died in 1810, left a bequest whereby forty dozen penny loaves were to be thrown from the church leads at twelve oclock on Christmas Day for ever. This is the latest instance of a scrambling custom with which we are acquainted. Bells were frequently cast in churchyards, and from the editor of this volume we have received some interesting notes on this subject. " In the days of the early bell founders," says Mr. William Andrews, " the country roads were little better than miry lanes, full of ruts and holes, and where the moisture of the winter was often not evaporated during the summer. For this reason bells were mostly cast in the immediate vicinity of the churches, or monastic establishments, they were intended to grace. The monks, too, were not unwilling to retain the usage as an opportunity for a religious service; they stood round the casting pit, and, as the metal was poured into the mould, would chant psalms and offer prayers. Southey, in The Doctor, says:—The brethren stood round the furnace, ranged in processional order, sang the 15Oth Psalm, and then, after certain prayers, blessed the molten metal, and called upon the Lord to infuse into it His grace, and overshadow it with His power, for the honour of the saint to whom the bell was to be dedicated, and whose name it was to bear.

Andrews " Curiosities of the Church."

Andrews " Curiosities of the Church," p. 89.

"Sometimes the bells were cast in the interior of the building, as at St. Albans, where, in the beginning of the I4th century, the great bell called the Amphibalus, being broken, was cast in the hall of the sacristy. In some places, Kirkby Malzeard, and Haddenham, for instance, the bells were cast in the church itself. But most frequently the churchyard was chosen for the purpose. At Scalford, during excavations made some time ago, there were found traces of a former furnace, and also a mass of bell metal, which had evidently been melted on the spot; about 1876, the churchyard of Empingham yielded a similar instance. The bells of Meaux Abbey were cast within the precincts. Coming down to more recent times we find the bell-founders obviating risks of transit by the same means. The Great Tom of Lincoln, in 1610, and the great bell of Canterbury, in 1762, were cast in the yards of their respective cathedrals. It was customary also for bell craftsmen to settle awhile in a particular locality, and thence extend their business from that centre to the churches around. This was done in 1734 by Daniel Hedderly, of Bawtry, at Winterton, in Lincolnshire, and by Henry Bagley, who advertised in 1732, that he would cast any ring or rings of bells in the town they belong." Latterly, however, the improved roads and means of transit have enabled bells to be cast in their proper foundries, and then conveyed to their posts of office."

Sundials were most commonly placed on the south wall of the church, but many a churchyard is graced by these obsolete time-keepers. At Kilham, East Yorkshire, opposite the door of the south porch of the church, a stone coffin has been sunk, head foremost, about half its length in the ground, and on the foot of this coffin a sundial was placed in 1769, and is still in a good state of preservation.

Wimborne Minster, Dorset, boasts a dial which must not be missed. It is dated 1732, and is to be found under the yew tree in the Minster yard, though its original position was on the gable of the north transept. It is of stone, 6 ft. in height; its south face is 4 ft. in width, and its east and west faces 3 ft. respectively, each of which bears a gnomon—a somewhat unusual feature.

A few miles from Canterbury, in Chilham churchyard, stands a beautiful sundial, the graceful stone pedstal of which was designed by the famous Inigo Jones.

Sundials have become well nigh useless owing to improved methods of keeping time, but one loves to see these relics which link us to a past which, with all its disadvantages, has many pleasant bye-paths for the men of to-day.

The stocks were sometimes placed in the churchyard, though more frequently near the village cross or in the market place. In 1578, tenpence was paid "for a hinging locke to the stockes in the Mynster Yearde," and again in 1693 "for rebuilding the gallows in the Horse faire, and the stocks in the Minster yard, 5s. iod." The stocks at Beverley Minster were movable, and placed in the yard when required for use.

York Fabric Rolls, p. n6.

A strange scene was enacted in St. Pauls churchyard, in May, 1531. According to Fox, the well known writer on martyrs, Bishop Stokesley "caused all the New Testament of Tyndals translation, and many other books which he had bought, to be openly burnt in St. Pauls churchyard."

A curious act of penance was performed in Hull, in 1534, by the vicar of North Cave. He had made a study of the work of the Reformers, who had settled in Antwerp, and sent their books over to England. In a sermon preached in the Holy Trinity Church, Hull, he advocated their teaching, and for this he was tried for heresy and convicted. He recanted, and as an act of penance, one Sunday, he walked round the church barefooted, with only his shirt on, and carrying a large faggot in his hand to represent the punishment he deserved.

Crosses have always been deemed a fitting emblem and suitable ornament for churchyards. Many ancient, interesting, and valuable crosses are yet to be found, notably at Ilkley, Crowle, Bakewell, and Eyam, the latter of which lay in pieces in a corner of the churchyard, until restored by John Howard, the philanthropist.

One result of church restoration by vicars, strangers to the place and people, and but newly installed, is the formation of a rubbish heap, in some neglected or unseen corner of the churchyard. Here are thrown, carelessly, cruelly, wantonly, costly stones of marble, alabaster, or granite, removed from the interior of the church, because there is no representative to plead for their safety. Boys clamber over the wall, make houses of the slabs, and for one brief hour, " dwell in marble halls," then go home and carry off the smaller pieces to ornament a rockery. It has been my good fortune, on more than one occasion, to rescue a monumental slab from destruction, and place it in the hands of the present representative of the family mentioned thereon.

Let us go through this little wicket gate which gives entrance to this village church-yard. As the gate clicks behind us, we find ourselves close to a handsome modern cross, raised on four circular steps. Here let us sit awhile and find rest for body and soul. The grass is closely cut between the graves, the little grassy mounds themselves have been made into tiny flower gardens. All around is evidence of care and pride in work; it is somebodys hobby as well as his living. Round the larger family graves, tasteful iron railings are fixed, and creeping plants and climbing roses rob the erection of its rigidity. At the beginning of the eighth century, a wise Northumbrian monarch was laid to rest in this " garden of sleep," and for twelve centuries the long roll of those joining the majority has been added to here in this quiet place, until the very dust on which we walk is sacred. Like Moses in the desert we are on holy ground–it is "Gods Acre."

altars in Cburcbes.

By The Rev. Geo. S. Tyack, B. a.

THE altar, although it is the most important and most conspicuous article of church furniture, is not one that provides much material for gossip of the quaint and curious kind. And this is natural: a decent reverence having protected the Christian " Holy of Holies" from the vagaries that have sometimes invented grotesque customs in connection with other parts of the church. This feeling of sanctity arises most obviously from the fact that on the altar the sacred mystery of the Eucharist is offered; but in early times it was intensified by the knowledge that beneath that altar rested the remains of some saint or martyr. In the first ages it was so far customary thus to commemorate the churchs departed heroes, that confessio, or martyrion (that is, the grave of a confessor or martyr), became recognized names for the altar.

I n later times the custom was reversed; the altar was no longer reared over the bones of the saint, but the body of anyone whom the church specially wished to honour was buried beneath the altar; and even now, when interments within churches are forbidden, the same natural feeling often finds expression in the burial of a parish priest immediately without the east wall, as near as possible to the altar that he served.

Probably it was the thought of security guaranteed by the sacredness of the altar which suggested to the monks of Canterbury the making of a grated vault beneath the high altar of the cathedral, in which to store their treasures. Here, before the Reformation, was kept a collection of gold and silver vessels, so large and costly, that in the opinion of Erasmus, Midas and Croesus would seem but beggars in presence of it. This altar was itself lavishly adorned, and all its glory had not disappeared in the days of Archbishop Laud, one of whose offences was the adorning of it with "a most idolatrous costly glory cloth."

For richness of material no altar that the world has seen could well excel the one erected in the Cathedral of S. Sophia by the Emperor Justinian. It was "a most inimitable work, for it was artificially composed of all sorts of materials that either the earth or the sea could afford, gold, silver, and all kinds of stones, wood, metals, and other things; which being melted and mixed together, a most curious table was framed out of this universal mass." The result, one cannot but think, with all its splendour, must have been somewhat barbaric. Other altars we read of in the early ages made of gold, or of pure silver, and others, like that presented to a church by Pulcheria according to Sozomen, adorned with gold and precious stones.

There seems never to have been any very definite rule in force as to the material of which an altar should be made. It is true that the Council of Epaone (a. d. 517) decreed that "no altar should be consecrated except it were of stone;" but in practice, metal and wooden altars still continued to be used, both in the east and the-west.

The custom of having a tabernacle permanently on the altar for the reservation of the Blessed Sacrament did not become usual until the twelfth century, but as early as the middle of the ninth century, Leo IV. mentions a pyx suspended for the same purpose above it. In fact we find traces as far back as the sixth of the use of pyxes in the form of doves made of gold or silver; and in England this custom continued until the Reformation. The pyx at Durham Cathedral, which hung from a hook still to be seen in the roof, was in the form of a pelican " in her piety," that is, feeding her young with her hearts blood; a figure which has been copied in the lectern now in use.

As the usual ornaments of the altar and its ministers became more numerous and more costly, it was inevitable that the question of responsibility for their provision should arise. Such a dispute came for settlement before Walter de Gray, Archbishop of York (1216-1256) in 1253, and he drew up a catalogue of such necessary things as the parishioners were to provide.

It will perhaps surprise some people to know that the custom of placing vases of flowers on the altar, so far from being a modern innovation, is one of the most ancient ways of adorning it. S. Augustine speaks of a young man taking a flower from an altar in an oratory dedicated to S. Stephen; and elsewhere we read of flowers, skilfully interwoven, as a decoration of the altar.

Anciently altars had no covering, except the linen clothes placed on the top, but as early as the sixth century Gregory of Tours speaks of a silk pall as a covering for one. It was in the eighth century, however, and by the influence of Pope Leo III., that altar-cloths came generally into use. The name for this in the Roman Missal is Pallium, or pall, and that name is still preserved in our English Coronation Service, where the gift of a pall is prescribed as part of the oblation to be made by the Sovereign. In accordance with this direction, and the custom of her ancestors, Queen Victoria, at her coronation, made an offering of a pall of cloth-of-gold, which was presented at the altar steps.

In marked contrast to the reverence shown to the altar in almost all ages and places, is a custom that for some couple of centuries existed at S. Ives in Huntingdonshire. A certain Dr. Robert Wilde, dying there in 1678, left a sum of "50, the interest of which was to be annually expended in the purchase of Bibles, each of which was not to exceed 7s. 6d. in price. The following extraordinary method of distributing these volumes was also enjoined. Six boys and six girls of the parish having been selected, were to stand at the altar and cast thereon with three dice, those making the highest aggregate number of points to have the Bibles. The occasion was to be further improved by the preaching of an appropriate sermon by the Vicar, for which he was to receive the sum of ios. A piece of ground, now known as " Bible Orchard," was bought with the legacy, and the distribution has duly taken place ever since in accordance with the donors wishes, except that in recent years a small table has been placed at the chancel step for the dice throwings, and the desecration of the altar avoided.

So strange a custom, however good the founders intention, could scarcely begin, much less take root, and live among us now; when we see on every hand efforts to treat Gods altar-throne with the reverence, and to adorn it with such dignity, as becomes it. And we may surely see in the revived life and widened usefulness of the English Church of to-day, a fulfilment of the Divine promise, "Them that honour Me, I will honour."

a be IRoofc loft anfc its Tflses.

By John T. Page.

"I HE word rood or rod is of Saxon origin, A and signifies a cross, or crucifix. It was universally adopted in Roman Catholic times to denote the cross on which Christ suffered death, and thus instead of the Holy Cross we invariably read of the Holy Rood.

The annals of legendary lore record that on the 3rd of May, A. d. 328, the true cross was found by St. Helena, buried deep in the ground at Jerusalem. Cosroes, King of Persia, on plundering the city, carried the precious relic away with him, but it was recovered again by Heraclius, Emperor of the Eastern Empire, who, in the year 629, made a pilgrimage to Jerusalem, and restored it to the Holy Sepulchre.

Ever since then the 14th of September has been celebrated as the Festival of the Holy Rood, or Holy Cross. Crosses had been set up in churches as far back as the year A. d. 431, and henceforward until the time of the Reformation they continued to be an important article of church furniture.

From the earliest times it had been customary to separate that part of the Church at the east end where the altar stood, from the body of the nave, where the common people assembled for worship. For this reason we find the arches between the chancel and the nave in Anglo-Saxon and Norman Churches very narrow, so that a curtain could easily be stretched across the opening. Later on this curtain was displaced by a screen of open woodwork, and in some cases stone was used instead of wood. This screen was generally carried up to the capitals of the columns which supported the chancel arch, and was surmounted by a substantial cross-beam. Upon the beam was constructed a loft or gallery, in the centre of which stood the rood, or crucifix. Access was generally gained to the rood loft by a newel staircase cut either in the north or south wall of the chancel, and occasionally ihe staircase existed on both sides. In some churches the rood loft extended across the side aisles as well, and this necessitated the erection of a specially constructed turret at the east end of one of the aisles.

The rood itself was always set in the centre of the loft, in such a position that it could be well seen by the assembled worshippers. Not only was the body of the Saviour represented as hanging upon the cross, but it was flanked on each side by attendant images of the Virgin Mary and St. John. These all faced the west, in accordance with a tradition that Christ was crucified with His face in that direction. It must not, however, be taken for granted that a rood loft existed in every church. Sometimes the rood was simply fixed on the cross-beam immediately over the screen, the gallery in this case being dispensed with.

It is a moot point as to when the rood was first set up in the English Church, but as there are scarcely any remains of screen-work of earlier date than the fourteenth century, it could not have been long before that time. There are, it is true, a few solitary specimens of thirteenth century work, but most of that which still exists is of fifteenth century date. Looking at examples of this period we generally find the rood loft projected a little forward over the screen, the angle thus formed being filled with groined work, springing from the protruding supports of the screen beneath. The upper part of the screen was filled with open work carving, which sometimes partook of the character of an elaborate symbolical design. The lower part was nearly always plain, but in conjunction with the upper surface was often elaborately painted and gilded.

When the Reformation came, the roods were all swept away by order, but the rood lofts in some cases became utilised as galleries for the singers. In the churchwardens account books, belonging to the parish of Stratton, Cornwall, under date 1549, occurs an entry of a sum of money-payd for takyng downe ye Rode and ye pagents yn ye rode lofte." It does not appear that any of the roods escaped destruction, but representations of the rood, and its attendant images of St. John and the Virgin Mary, were sometimes carved in. stone and inserted in the walls of churches, and of these a few still remain. It is therefore possible to obtain from these stone carvings a very good idea of how the rood looked when it was set up in the rood loft. Mr. Bloxam mentions examples at Romsey, Hants; Sherborne, Dorset; Burford, Oxon, and Evesham, Worcester; and the writer may add that a fine specimen is to be seen over the south doorway of Stepney Church, Middlesex.

It it presumed that an altar sometimes stood in the loft in front of the rood. The fact that at Maxey Church, Northamptonshire, a piscina is to be found in the south wall of the clerestory would seem to enforce such a theory. On special occasions lights and other decorations occupied a place in the loft near the rood. It has also been stated that the Gospel and Epistle, and various other parts of the service, were read from the rood loft.

Very good examples of a late Perpendicular rood screen and loft exist at Bugbrook Church, Northamptonshire. The screen consists of three compartments, of which the central one is the widest. It is ten feet seven inches high, and at the base of the loft, measures nineteen feet three inches across. The lower part of the central compartment, which went to form the doors, is missing. The upper part is arched, and down the centre of the arch runs a mullion. This description of the upper portion corresponds with the two side compartments, where, however, the mullions are continued down to the ground. The lower parts on each side are filled with plain panels, which have apparently been inserted in later times. A series of elaborate vaulting springs from the main supports of the structure, and upholds to the rood loft, which projects over the top of the screen. The vaulting is covered with fan tracery, the spaces between the ribs being filled in with a rich design. The loft is between three and four feet in width, and the cross beam on which it rests is seven inches wide. Admission to the loft is gained from the south side, through a narrow arched opening in the wall. The steps originally descended into the south aisle, but there are only five of them now remaining.

The counties of Devon and Somerset probably contain some of the finest examples of rood screens and rood lofts. On one at least of these the rood has lately been replaced, for in a recent number of Notes and Queries Mr. Harry Hems, of Exeter, writes as follows:–" The only rood screen I recollect for the moment having the three figures upon it, is at St. Andrews, Kenn. I placed them there some seven or eight years ago."

There seems now to be a general inclination towards a revival of the rood screen. Even in our most recently built churches, a temporary screen, festooned with flowers or other decorations, may often be seen erected on the occasion of harvest festivals, and such-like celebrations. Whether or no the setting up of the rood in the rood loft will ever again become customary in the English Church, is a question time alone can solve.

8th S. V. 150, Feb. 24, 1894.

Hrmour in Cburcbes.

By J. Charles Cox, Ll. d., F. s. a.

THE memorial brasses, the incised slabs, and especially the effigies of knights and men-at-arms, which abound in our churches, tell us far more of the successive stages and development of English arms and armour, both of an offensive and defensive character, than all the manuscript inventories or actual collections of weapons that are yet extant. And not only do our churches thus yield the most valuable and trustworthy evidence as to the armour of our forefathers, by its faithful pourtrayal on the memorials of the departed, but they also afford a sanctuary in numerous cases for actual armour.

It was for many centuries a custom of Christendom–apparently more particularly in England than elsewhere–to suspend over the tomb the principal arms of the departed warrior, which had previously been carried in the funeral procession. Hearne, the well-known antiquary of last century, says that the custom originated with Canute placing his crown upon the head of the crucifix at Winchester, when he found that the waves refused to obey him; but it is somewhat difficult to follow the reasoning which makes this a precedent for the hanging up of the dead mans armour.

The custom is twice noted by Shakespeare. In

"Hamlet," Laertes says:–

"His means of death, his obscure burial–
No trophy, sword, nor hatchment oer his bones,
No noble rite, nor formal ostentation."

Iden, in " Henry VI.," remarks:–

"Ist Cade that I have slain, that monstrous traitor,
Sword, I will hallow thee for this thy deed,
And hang thee oer my tomb, when I am dead."

The armour in our churches may be divided into two classes; firstly, that which had actually been worn by the person commemorated, and secondly, that which was specially constructed for funeral purposes.

The most deeply interesting and the oldest of genuine armour still preserved within English churches, is that which pertained to the Black Prince, and which hangs above his well-known tomb in the cathedral church of Canterbury. In June, 1894, this armour was exhibited at Burlington House, in the rooms of the Society of Antiquaries, when we had special opportunities of examining it. The great tilting helm of iron weighs seven pounds. The leathern cap inside it is almost worn away. The gilded long-tailed lion which forms the crest is of leather. The great shield of France and England quarterly is also of embossed leather. The gauntlets are oflatten, and still retain the inner leather gloves. The sword-scabbard and buckle are of the same material; the sword itself is unfortunately missing, and is said to have been appropriated by Oliver Cromwell when visiting Canterbury.

The surcoat, which laced up the back, is of velvet, and well padded. It is not a little remarkable that the arms of neither shield nor surcoat bear any label or mark of cadency, but are simply royal arms. Mr. St. John Hope ingeniously conjectures that this singular omission can only be accounted for on the supposition that the relics were really those of Edward III., and not of his son, the Black Prince, and that they were hung up over the sons tomb by the kings order as a mark of his deep affection.

At the same exhibition the actual shield of Henry V., from Westminster Abbey, was also shown.

Sir David Owen, by his will, dated February 20th, 1529, desires that "my body be buried in the priory of Esseborne, after the degree of a banneret, that is with helmet and sword, my war armour, my banner, my standard, and my pendant."

Sir Godfrey Foljambe, of Walton, by his will, in 1532, left his "carcase to be buried in the chappell of St. George besides my lady wife in Chesterfield. my sword, helmet, with the crest upon the head, and my coat-of-arms to be hanged over my tomb, and there to remain for ever."

Several of our parish churches still retain arms or armour or other accoutrements that had actually been worn by the person commemorated. Among them, to our own knowledge, may be mentioned Bonsall, Derbyshire; Brington, Northamptonshire; Addington, Surrey; Sheriff Hutton, Yorkshire; Broadwater, Sussex; St. Michael Carhayes, Cornwall; St. Mary Redcliffe, Bristol; Brabourne, Kent; and Longbridge Deverill, Wilts.

Occasionally, however, and particularly in the sixteenth and seventeenth centuries, the armour carried in the funeral procession, and subsequently suspended over the tomb, was merely supplied by the undertaker or heraldic official, and was of a cheap and imitative character, not intended to last. Sir William Dugdale states (in 1667) the actual price of such sham armour. A knights helmet, gilt with silver and gold, was ; the crest, carved and coloured, 13s.; the sword, with velvet scabbard, los.; gauntlets, Ids. ; and gilt spurs, 5s. Light helmets and breastplates of this funeral-trophy description, from which all gilt and beauty has long since disappeared, are still to be found in some of our churches, and occasionally may be seen among discarded lumber in parvises, as at Raunds, Northamptonshire.

There is, however, a yet more important aspect of armour in churches to be considered. Every parish in England, from the time of Edward I. downwards, was bound to keep ready for use a certain amount of armour, and a man or men, according to the population of the township, properly trained to the use of this armour. This armour had to be viewed twice a year by the constables, and a report as to its condition made to the justices. Not infrequently, when a suit able " church-house " was wanting, the

" townes armour" of our English villages, and even of country towns, was kept in the church itself, particularly in the parvise or room over the porch.

When the parish armour was carefully viewed throughout England at the time of the expected Spanish invasion in the reign of Elizabeth, returns show that much of it was in safe quarters within the consecrated walls of our churches. We have met with various instances of inventories or mention of " townes armour" in old constable accounts. One of the fullest of these is in the parish books of Repton, Derbyshire. In 1590 is this entry:–

"A Note of the armoure of Repton receaved into the handes of Rycharde Weatte, berjinge Constable.

Imprimis ij corsletts wth all that belongeth unto them.

It. ij platt cotts (coats of plate armour).

It. ij swordes and iij daigers and ij gyrgells.

It. ij calevers wth flaxes and tuch boxe.

It ij pyckes and ij halberds.

It. for the TYband Souldiar a cote and bowe and a shiffe of arrowes and a quiver."

In 1616, the inventory is as follows:– -" Receaved by Christopher Ward Constable from John Couttrell the Townes Armore.

2 Corsletts with 2 pickes.

2 Culivers.

One flask and tuch boxe.

V headpeeces; towe of them ould ones.

2 howlboardes.

One payre of Banddelrowes.

2 oulde girdles.

3 new girdles; towe of them with ye sowldiers.

3 payre of hanggers in the sowldiers keepinge.

3 swordes with towe daggers.

Allsoe the swordes in sowldiers keepinge.

Allsoe 2 platte coottes y Clocksmith not delivered."

This armour was kept in the parish church at Repton; up to the year 1840 some of it still remained in the parvise or room over the south porch.

In the first year of Elizabeth, it is recorded that there was in the parish church of Darley, Derbyshire, " within ye steepul both harnes and weapons in redynes for one billman and for one archer."

In Cussans county history of Hertfordshire, it is recorded that some "twenty years ago," the south porch of Baldock church was enlarged by removing the floor of the parvise. This chamber, which had remained closed for many years, was found to be nearly filled with armour, helmets, pikes, and other weapons, It was assumed by Cussans that this was a collection of armour, heaped together from tombs over which they had been suspended, but there can be no doubt it was merely the old store of towns armour.

Beating tbe Skmtands.

By John T. Page.

IN those early days, when deities were called into existence at the sweet will of every potentate, we note the fact that somewhere between the years 715-672 B. c., King Numa Pompilius introduced to the Roman citizens, the worship of the god Terminus. He originated a plan, by which the fields of the citizens were separated from each other by means of boundary stones, which stones were dedicated, and made sacred to the god Terminus. The Terminalia, as the festival of Terminus was called, was celebrated annually on the 23rd of February. On this day the people turned out in force, and visiting the different boundary stones, decked them with flowers, and performed sacrificial rites amid great rejoicings.

From the seventh century B. c., to the end of the nineteenth century of the Christian era is a long stride, but it is pretty generally considered that in this annual Terminalia of the ancient Romans, we have the germ of the custom known as " Beating the Bounds," which in many parishes throughout England is still carried out annually.

The early Christians readily adapted some of the best heathen customs to their own requirements, and thus we soon find them making a perambulation round their fields, accompanied by their bishops and clergy. They repeated litanies, and implored God to avert plague and pestilence, and to enable them in due season to reap the fruits of the earth. "The Litanies or Rogations then used gave the name of Rogation Week to this time. They occur as early as the 55Oth year of the Christian era, when they were first observed by Mamertius, Bishop of Vienna, on account of the frequent earthquakes that happened, and the incursions of wild beasts, which laid in ruins and depopulated the city."t

Some idea of the importance which eventually came to be attached to this Rogation time, may be gathered from an old sermon, still extant, in which the preacher, after animadverting upon a growing misuse of the festival by certain people, tells ihem that for this cause "it is merveyle God destroye us not in one daye,"–and then proceeds as follows:–" In these Rogation Days, it is to be asked of God, and prayed for, that God of his goodness wyll defende and save the corne in the felde, and that he wyll vouchsave to pourge the ayer. For this cause be certaine Gospels red in the wide, felde amonges the corne and grasse, that by the vertue and operation of Gods word, the power of the wicked spirites, which kepe in the air and infecte the same (whence come pestilences and the other kyndes of diseases and syknesses) may be layde downe, and the aier made pure and cleane, to th intent the corne may remaine unharmed, and not infected of the sayd hurteful spirites, but serve us for our use and bodely sustenaunce."

In some parishes a Triennial or even Septennial visit to the boundaries is considered sufficient.

t Brand.

In order that we may now get a better idea of what these processions were like, we cannot do better than turn to Shaws History of Staffordshire We there learn that "Among the local customs which have prevailed (at Wolverhampton), may be noticed that which was popularly called Processioning. Many of the older inhabitants can well remember when the sacrist, resident prebendaries, and members of the choir, assembled at Morning Prayers on Monday and Tuesday in Rogation Week, with the charity children, bearing long poles clothed with all kinds of flowers then in season, and which were afterwards carried through the streets of the town with much solemnity, the clergy, singing men and boys, dressed in their sacred vestments, closing the procession, and chanting in a grave and appropriate melody, the Canticle, Benedicite Omnia Opera, etc. It was discontinued about

Vol. ii., part i., p. 165.

1765."

In the seventeenth century mention is often made of the Rogation week processions in the Articles of Enquiry in the different Archdeaconries. As an example we may cite the following from the Archdeaconry of Middlesex, under date 1662. " Doth your minister or curate, in Rogation Dayes, go in Perambulation about your Parish, saying and using the Psalms and Suffrages by Law appointed, as viz., Psalm 103 and 104, the Letany and Suffrages, together with the Homily, set out for that end and purpose? Doth he admonish people to give thanks to God, if they see any likely hopes of plenty, and to call upon him for mercy, if there be any fear of scarcity: and do you, the Churchwardens, assist him in it?"

The judicious Hooker would by no means omit the customary time of Procession, persuading all, both rich and poor, if they desired the preservation of love and their parish rights and liberties, to accompany him in his Perambulation: and most did so: in which Perambulation he would usually express more pleasant discourse than at other times, and would then always drop some loving and facetious observations, to be remembered against the next year, especially by the boys and young people."

As might have been expected, some very curious entries appear in the churchwardens books of different parishes relative to expenses incurred on the occasion of the annual procession. From the parish books of St. Margaret, Westminster, the following have been culled:–

"1555. Item, paid for spiced bread on the Ascension-Even, and on the Ascension Day, 1s."

"1556. Item, paid for bread, wine, ale, and beer, upon the Ascension-Even and Day, against my Lord Abbott and his Covent cam in Procession, and for strewing herbs the samme day, 7s. 1d."

"1559. Item, for bread, ale, and beer, on Tewisday in the Rogacion Weeke, for the parishioners that went in Procession, is."

"Waltons Life."

"1560. Item, for bread and drink for the parishioners that went the Circuit the Tuesday in the Rogation

Week, 33. 4d."

"Item, for bread and drink the Wednesday in the

Rogation Week, for Mr. Archdeacon and the Quire of the Minster, 3s. 4d." " 1585. Item, paid for going the Perambulacion, for fish, butter, cream, milk, conger, bread and drink, and other necessaries, 4s. 8j4d." " 1597. Item, for the charges of diet at Kensington for the Perambulation of the Parish, being a yeare of great scarcity and deerness, 6 8s. 8d." " 1605. Item, paid for bread, drink, cheese, fish, cream, and other necessaries, when the worshipfull and others of the parish went the Perambulation to

Kensington,

By way of accessories, the customs of " whipping " and "bumping" gradually came to form part of the perambulation ceremony. In order that the boundaries of the parishes might be indelibly impressed on the minds of the younger portion of the community, it was deemed advisable to bump some promising boy painfully against the boundary stones; or better still, to publicly whip him while he strove to impress on his memory the exact position of the same landmarks.

As a set off against this public humiliation, the boys had a present of money given to them, and accordingly there appears an entry in the Chelsea parish books, in 1670, as follows:–

"Given to the boys that were whipt, 4s."

The process of "bumping" has been carried on until quite recently, for on June 8th, 1881, the Guardian reported a case in which three men who were engaged in "Beating the Bounds" were fined,5 each for forcibly " bumping" the senior curate of Hanwell. They met the curate and "asked him to go and be bumped. Upon his declining, two of the defendants took hold of his arms and dragged him to the stone, one of the party taking him by the leg and lifting him bodily from the ground. On reaching the stone, they bumped him against a man."

It. would take too long to mention all the numerous observances which still linger on in various places in connection with this ancient and interesting custom. In most parishes where it is still kept up, the ceremony is performed annually on Ascension Day. A friend of the writer thus describes the way in which it is carried out in one of the outlying districts of London:–

Lysons " Lon. ion, ii, 126.

"We assembled, by invitation, at the Vestry Hall, about to oclock a. m. I should think there were thirty or forty gentlemen present, including the rector, churchwardens, and various officers of the parish, and about the same number of schoolboys. The gentlemen wore rosettes, and carried rods, and the boys were provided with long willow wands decked with blue ribbons. The parish beadle, carrying the mace, marched in front. When we came to any of the boundary stones of the parish, they were duly examined to see if they were in their proper position, and then the boys gave three cheers, and beat them with their wands. We marched through private houses and warehouses, over walls, ditches, canals, etc., and were taken down the river in a barge, until at last we came to our starting-point again about 4-30 in the afternoon. The churchwardens then presented each of the boys with a new shilling and dismissed them."

In these days of ordnance maps, there may be very little practical utility in " Beating the Bounds," but as Wordsworth says:–

"Many precious relics
And customs of our rural ancestry
Are gone or stealing from us."

Time is ever busy blotting out the land-marks which our ancestors reared with so much patience for our behoof. It is well, therefore, if occasionally, with reverential spirit, we try to set in order the fragments of those that still remain. In so doing, we may perchance cull some useful lesson, and ere they pass away for ever, haply profit by the experiences which they record.

Gfoc Story of tbc Crosier.

By The Rev. Geo. S. Tyack, B. a.

THE staff of authority, which we have in so many forms, as sceptre, crosier, mace, wand, or otherwise, has its origin in each case in one of two ideas. Sometimes it is an instrument of correction; thus the churchwardens staff, the wand or rod of a royal usher, and of a beadle, and probably also the mace of a mayor, were all, like the fasces of a Roman governor, intended to correct the unruly, or to forcibly clear a way, when necessary, for the progress of the dignitary before whom they were borne. In other cases this symbol of authority, as it has now become, was originally nothing more or less than the trusty staff on which the aged ruler leaned, as on a modern walking stick. All language points to the fact that age was at first considered an essential condition of dignity and authority, for almost all terms of respect imply the seniority of the person addressed. Sir, sieur or monsieur, signor, senor, are of course but varied forms of the word senior/ and we have more particular instances in the terms sire, senator, and alderman, in matters of state, with patriarch, father (applied to a bishop or a priest) and pope, abbot, priest, presbyter, or elder, in the Church. Thus it came to pass that in the earliest times the aged ruler was usually seen supporting his weight of years by the help of his staff; and the step from this familiar sight to the idea that the staff symbolized his rule, was simple and natural. The sceptre, therefore, which was the needful support of Homers old councillors, has become the emblem of royal power; and the crutch-stick of the aged bishop is transfigured into the crosier.

This being the case, it is obviously impossible to fix the exact date at which the crosier, or any other of these staves of office, came to be recognized simply as such, the progress from the first idea being in all cases a gradual development. We find the episcopal staff, however, mentioned in connection with S. Caesarius of Aries, who was bishop of that See from A. n. 501 to 542, and it is also referred to by Gregory, Bishop of Tours, in the same century, and again in the proceedings of the Fourth Council of Toledo a little later.

In primitive times it was made of wood, usually of elder, or, as some say, of cypress, and in the form of a T; and the name expressive of that shape seems to have lingered long, at least in England. Pilkington, Bishop of Durham, from 1561 to 1577, speaks once and again of the " cruche and mitre." But as the symbolical idea grew and the wealth of the church increased, the staff naturally became handsomer in design and materials, as being expressive of the episcopal dignity. Jewels and the precious metals were employed in its adornment, and comparatively soon it assumed the crook shape, now its universal form, significant of the office of the Bishop as the Chief Shepherd of his diocese. In the Eastern Church the curved staff is said to be reserved for the Patriarchs.

The pastoral idea of the clerical, and especially of the episcopal office, probably arose from our Lords assumption of the title of "the Good Shepherd," and was further emphasized by His charge to S. Peter, "Feed My sheep, feed My lambs." In allusion to this, the figure of the Saviour presenting that Apostle with a crooked staff is familiar in Art, and the thought finds expression in several writers of the English Church. Jewell, Bishop of Salisbury (1560-1571) writes, "Their crosiers staff signifies diligence in attending the flock of Christ," and William Tyndale speaks of "that Shepherds crook, the bishops cross." More authoritative is the allusion in the Ordinal, where, at the consecration of a bishop, the rubric runs, "Then shall the

Archbishop put into his hand the pastoral staff, saying, Be to the flock of Christ a shepherd, not a wolf, feed them, devour them not." The words still stand in our prayer-books, although the accompanying significant act has not been enjoined since the first book of Edward VI., of 1549.

Most of the early examples of the use of the crosier in England are found in the carvings of bishops tombs. We have, for instance, in their Cathedral the effigies of Bartholomew of Exeter, Bishop of that diocese from 1161 to 1184, bearing a staff, the butt of which pierces a dragon at-his feet; and of Simon of Apulia, who followed in the same See in 1214 to 1224, with the same insignia. Other figures might be mentioned at York, Salisbury, Worcester, Wells, and indeed in most of our Cathedrals, the form of the crosier varying little in the several cases, except in richness of design. The curious and more than questionable custom of making, in a kind of sport, a Boy Bishop, is commemorated at Salisbury by the tomb of one such, whose effigy bears the crosier along with the other marks of his sham dignity.

The finest specimen of an ancient staff still preserved among us, is that of William of Wykeham, Bishop of Winchester (1367-1405), bequeathed by that great prelate himself to New College, Oxford.

After the Reformation, in the general decline of ceremonial and symbolism, the pastoral staff and the mitre fell alike into disuse in England, surviving only as senseless decorations, or heraldic additions to the tombs or arms of bishops, who had never used either the one or the other, had perhaps never even seen them. At the present time the use of the crosier has once more become almost universal in the English dioceses, and the added dignity of the mitre promises soon to be scarcely less frequently found.

But besides the bishops, the abbots of the most important monastic foundations formerly bore and wore crosier and mitre in token of their authority, the mark of difference being that while the bishop had his crosier carried with the crook turned outwards as a sign of his rule over the whole diocese, the abbot carried his, usually one of simpler design, crook inwards, to signify the purely domestic or internal character of his government.

The English mitred abbots sat and voted in the House of Lords until the dis-solution of their communities under Henry VIII. They were the heads of the following abbeys, namely, S. Albans, Glastonbury, Westminster, Bury S. Edmunds, Bardney, Shrewsbury, Crowland, Abington, Eve-sham, Gloucester. Ramsey, York (S. Marys), Tewkesbury, Reading, Battle, Winchcourt, Hide-by-Winchester, Cirencester, Waltham, Thorney, Canterbury (S. Augustines), Selby, Peterborough, Colchester (S. Johns), and Tavistock, twenty-five in all, of which the last was considerably the latest addition to the list.

One of the earliest examples of the abbatial staff in England is on the tomb of Abbot Vitalis (died 1082) in the cloister of Westminster Abbey, and another early instance of its use is supplied by the effigy of Abbot Andrew (1193-1200) in Peterborough Cathedral. Parker, the last Abbot of Gloucester, lies buried in the Cathedral there, and Philip Ballard de Hanford, the last Abbot of Evesham, in Worcester Cathedral, each with his crosier.

Before leaving this subject an effort should be made to remove a misconception. A common modern fallacy is that there is a distinction between the crosier and the pastoral staff, the latter name being assigned to the crook of a bishop, and the former to the processional cross borne before an Archbishop. The late Dean Hook, if he was not the originator of the idea in an article in his " Church Dictionary," at any rate did much to propagate it thereby, and it is now frequently found in books of reference. But the use of the words in the past is all against it. It is true that crosier comes from the Latin crux, a cross, but from the same root too, come crook and crutch; so that nothing can be proved from the derivation. It would seem that the original form of the word was erase, as it is given in a quotation used above, whence the chaplain who bore it was a crosier. From this it became the crosiers staff, the crosier-staff, and finally the crosier; all having reference to the crook of Episcopal Authority.

Btsbops in Battle.

By Edward Lamplough.

AFTER William, Duke of Normandy, came in with great toil and rout of war, on Senlacs evil day, it was not difficult to apply the poets lines to many a proud prelate of the Anglo-Norman eppch:–

"Princely was his hand in largess, heavy was his arm to smite, And his will was leaded iron, like the mace he bore in fight."

Not that English Bishops had not found it necessary to take the field in pre-conquest times, when the old Danish wars convulsed the island, and the inhabitants suffered severely from the unbridled passion and cruelty of a barbarous and heathen soldiery.

Many a grand old Anglo-Saxon prelate found himself called upon as a Christian and a patriot to take his station in the van of the kings army, to bar the path of the invader, and fence with sword and spear the ancient churches and the fruitful plains of his beloved island.

The old English chroniclers have preserved for us the names of a few of those warrior bishops. Ealstan, Bishop of Sherborne, may be specially referred to. A. d. 823, he assisted Prince Ethel-wulf during an expedition into Kent, and in 845 he was one of the commanders in the great victory over the Danes at the mouth of the Parret. He died, full of years and honours, in that unhappy and troublous 867, having held the Bishopric of Sherborne fifty years. His successor, Bishop Heahmund, was not so fortunate; he fought under Ethelred and Alfred during the sanguinary and disastrous campaign of 871, and was slain at Marden, when victory remained with the Danes. When Edmund Ironsides encountered Canute at Assingdon, and was betrayed by that infamous traitor Edric Streon, among those who swelled the huge death-mounds was Ednoth, Bishop of Dorchester, and Abbot Wulsy, but Hoveden asserts that "they had come for the purpose of invoking the Lord on behalf of the soldiers."

Another Bishop of Sherborne was slain on the eve of Brunnanburgh, A. d. 937. When the two armies were within striking distance, and prepared for what was certain to prove a sanguinary and stubborn conflict, Anlaf, disguised as a harper, entered the lines of Athelstans army, and, by the merit of his performance, was admitted into the royal presence, and received several pieces of gold in reguerdon of his skill. Too proud to carry away his minstrels fee, he secreted it beneath the turf, before passing out of the camp. During the performance he had been narrowly scrutinised by one of Athelstans soldiers, who had formerly served the Northumbrian Prince, and was suspicious that the talented minstrel was no other than the warlike Anlaf. After witnessing Anlafs disposal of his fee, his suspicion was confirmed, and he hurried to Athelstan to warn him of the danger that might result from Anlafs visit. His having once sworn fealty to the Northumbrian Prince was alleged as a sufficient reason for not betraying him into the kings hands, and Athelstan readily accepted the explanation. Nevertheless, he removed his tent to a distant and less exposed position; and when, some time afterward, the Bishop of Sherborne arrived, with his contingent of warriors, he pitched his tent on the recently vacated ground. That night, when the watch-fires burnt low, and, save the weary sentinels, the royal army was buried in slumber, Anlaf burst in with sword and spear, and a sudden storm of midnight battle convulsed the whole camp. After a fierce struggle the enemy was driven out, but when day dawned the Bishop of Sherborne was found, cold and still, in the midst of the slain.

Such was the nature of the military service of the church during the pre-conquest period, and similar service was not infrequently rendered after the Normans came in, when sudden storms of invasion swept across the Scottish borders, to burst on the dark and bloody battle-ground of Northumbria.

With the memorable battle of Northallerton, or the Standard, A. d. 1138, the church was in a very special degree connected, and indeed the priesthood had suffered severely from the barbarous Scotch. Thus Wendover, "they slew priests upon the altars, cut off the heads of the crucifixes, and placed them on the decapitated corpses, putting in their places the bloody heads of their victims; wherever they went, it was one scene of cruelty and terror; women shrieking, old men lamenting, and every living being in despair." The evil grew so intolerable that the aged Thurston, Archbishop of York, incited the northern barons to unite against the enemy, exerting himself with almost superhuman energy to organise the movement, appealing to the religious feelings of the people by processions of the clergy, by sermons and exhortations, and when the army arrayed itself for battle, its serried ranks surrounded the famous standard, " consisting of the mast of a ship securely lashed to a four-wheeled car or wain. On the summit of this mast was placed a large crucifix, having in its centre a silver box containing the consecrated host, and below it waved the banners of the three patron saints:–Peter of York, Wilfred of Ripon, and John of Beverley." Thurston, incapacitated from being present by the infirmities of age, had delegated Ralph Nowel, the titulary Bishop of Orkney, to act for him, and he it was, according to the old writers who exhorted the army to make a brave defence when the Scots bore down upon them, and the dreadful conflict commenced. The battle resulted in a glorious victory for the Anglo-Norman men- at-arms and the peasant archers of Northumbria, but the name of Archbishop Thurston is always primarily and honourably associated with this memorable event.

Under somewhat similar circumstances, A. d. 1319, William de Melton, Arch- bishop of York, seconded by the Mayor, Nicholas Fleming, hastily raised a tumultuary army of 10,000 men, burghers and peasants, necessarily undisciplined and ill-armed, and utterly unfitted to dispute the field with a powerful and veteran army, marching under Bruces most experienced and fortunate captains, Randolph and Douglas. The armies struck at My ton Meadows, near the confluence of the Swale and Ure, on September the 13th. With everything in their favour the Scots resorted to ambuscade, and, sweeping down upon the startled enemy, in an instant covered the field with dead and wounded men, driving before them a wild rout of fugitives. Sir Nicholas

Fleming, then in the seventh year of his mayoralty, was slain; it was with the utmost difficulty that the Archbishop effected his escape, for the Scots spared none, and night alone covered the remnant of the army from the exterminating sword. Nearly 4,000 of the Englishmen were destroyed, including 300 priests, attired in full canonicals, from which tragic circumstance the rude Scots jestingly referred to the battle as the " Chapter of Mitton."

The bearer of the Archbishops cross secreted it on the field, and it fell into the hands of a peasant, who, for some days, concealed it in his hut, no doubt tempted by its value, but conscience operated so powerfully that the good fellow was constrained to restore it to the Archbishop.

A dour revenge the English Bishops took upon their Scottish adversaries in 1346, when King Edward was encamped before Calais, and luckless David Bruce came over the border with 50,000 men at his back, in the month of October. Queen Philippa bestirred herself with heroic energy on this occasion, and marched with the army to the north. It was largely swollen by the vassals of the church. The Bishop of Durham commanded in the first division; William de la Zouche, Archbishop of York, and the Bishop of Carlisle, led the second division; the Bishop of Lincoln the third; and the Archbishop of Canterbury the fourth. Edward Baliol and the principal nobles of Northumbria shared the command with the prelates.

During the furious struggle that ensued the monks of Durham assembled on the rising ground known as the Maidens Bower, and knelt in prayer around the banner-cloth of St. Cuthbert, or occupied themselves in manufacturing a fair wooden cross, as a memorial of the event.

The battle terminated in a signal triumph to the English army, despite the distin-guished valour of the Scottish host, and the closing scene was one of peculiar interest. Almost alone amid the wreck of the field, David Bruce disdained to surrender, al-though " he had two spears hanging in his body, his leg almost incurably wounded, and his sword beaten out of his hand," and John Copeland, a sturdy Northumbrian squire, was bent upon his capture, and ultimately succeeded in carrying him off in triumph to his castle of Ogle, but not until the fiery Scot had dashed out two of his teeth by a buffet of his gauntleted fist.

Most unsaintly, perhaps, of all the English bishops who loved the music of twanging bowstrings and clashing steel, was " Weymundus or Reymundus," first Bishop of Sodar and Man. When a monk of Furness Abbey he was famous as an illuminator and transcriber of MSS.; but accompanying several of the brethren on a mission to the Isle of Man, the rude Manxmen were so deeply impressed by his eloquence, dignity, and commanding stature, that they procured his elevation to the Bishopric.

Wymund the Saxon, as the Bishop is generally called, was incited by an unworthy ambition to claim the crown of Scotland, then worn by David I. Assuming the name of Malcolm Macbeth, he gave out that he was the son of Angus, Earl of Moray, recently slain at the battle of Strickathrow, and who was the heir of Macbeths son and successor, Leelach. Obtaining a number of large boats, he repeatedly attacked the neighbouring islands, finding numerous intrepid and desperate adventurers ready to follow him for love of adventure and plunder. He soon made his name widely known and feared, and Somerled, Lord of the Isles, was induced to bestow upon him the hand of his daughter, who bore him a son, Donald Macbeth. Knights and men-at-arms were despatched to foil his invasions of the mainland, but by availing himself of forest and mountain fastnesses, he avoided his more powerful enemies, escaping by his boats when hard pressed. Many of the bishops paid him black-mail, but one tough old prelate, a man after his own heart, met him in open field, axe in hand, and smote him to the earth, and defeated and scattered his following. Wymund escaped, however, and soon took the field again.

Ultimately David pacified the claimant by a grant of lands, and Wymund returned to the Isle of Man, or, according to William of Newbridge, to the Abbey of Furness, where his severities so enraged the monks that they fell on him, bound him, and destroyed his sight and virility. He was then handed over to King David, who shut him up in Roxburgh Castle, but, after some years, transferred him to Byland Abbey, where his stories of adventure by land and sea long delighted the good fathers.

Somerled, endeavouring to maintain the claim of Wymunds son, was slain in battle near Renfrew, by the Lord High Steward and the Earl of Angus. The wicked and vexatious claims of Wymund were terminated in 1164 by the capture and imprisonment of his son.

The necessities of the times justified many of the prelates in assuming arms, and Wymund must be regarded as an exceptional character, neither true priest nor bishop. Nevertheless several of the English bishops appear to have been quite willing to make arms a profession, while others, as Odo, Bishop of Bayeux, combined the ecclesiastical and baronial offices, employing both in the furtherance of their personal ambition. When the Conqueror arrested his ambitious half-brother, it will be remembered that he arrested him not as the churchman, but as the Earl of Kent.

Odo was a principal figure, with Geoffrey, Bishop of Coutance, at Senlac, when the Norman Duke conquered Harolds crown; and he was held in well-deserved reprobation for the sanguinary revenge that he exacted for the slaying of Walcher, Bishop of Durham, and his following of a hundred French and Flemish men-at-arms, at Gateshead, on the 14th of May, 1080.

The death of the Conqueror let Odo loose upon society again, and he returned to England, where he was well received by Rufus, and his forfeited estates restored. His unprincipled ambition, and his rage against Archbishop Lanfranc, induced him to organise a conspiracy against the king, in which he was supported by Bishop Gosfrith, William, Bishop of Durham, and a number of the Anglo-Norman nobles. Raising a Saxon army, Rufus reduced Tunbridge and Pevensey Castles, in the latter of which he secured the arch-traitor. Nevertheless Odo was permitted to proceed to Rochester Castle, for the purpose of opening negotiations. The bravest of the revolted nobles occupied the fortress, and Odo remained with them, a willing captive, but the ruse deceived no one. After a tedious siege the castle was compelled to surrender, and Odo issued forth, amid sounding trumpets, and the menaces of the English soldiery, to depart over sea, with the bitter curses of the islanders ringing in his ears. The Bishop of Durham was also reduced to extremities, and, with many of the revolted Normans, sent after Odo, as the Anglo-Saxon Chronicle records.

Men of Odos stamp were not wanting among the bishops, when Stephen seized the crown, barely seventy years after the Battle of Hastings, when the direct male line of the Conqueror failed. During the period of almost unparalleled suffering that followed, bishops were seen in the hostile camps, leading the mercenary soldiery, and even gambling for their share of the spoils collected by those ruthless marauders. They were armed in complete mail, bore truncheon and lance, and bestrode heavy war-steeds, like warlike knights and captains of the mercenaries.

Henry, Bishop of Winchester, acted a prominent part in the war between Stephen and Matilda, changing sides as policy and ambition dictated, and when, after the revolt of the

Londoners, he again espoused his brothers cause, he had to retire from Winchester, leaving Matilda in the possession of the castle, while her troops closely invested the episcopal palace. He speedily re-entered Winchester with a considerable force at his back, and Matildas soldiery rushed in confusion to the churches, which they essayed to defend. The Bishop was not to be denied, and to avoid the long and dubious strife, and heavy loss of life that would attend the storming of the holy edifices, he set fire to them, and afterwards gave his undivided attention to the castle, which he reduced to extremities, after a leaguer of six weeks, but the ex-empress effected her escape.

With reference to the military proclivities of our bishops, it is due to them to point out that as councillors and ambassadors they were naturally in great request at court, where their superior education and training enabled them to serve the state and crown to advantage. The nation was continually at war, kings and courtiers were warriors, hence the bishops were accustomed to both court and camp, and vied with the proudest baron in the splendour of their apparel, and the number of their attendant knights and men-at-arms.

The following brief extract from Hallam, relating to feudal tenures in Anglo-Saxon England, throws some little light on the military service of some of the bishops in pre-conquest times, although, no doubt, many churchmen considered it a holy war that they waged against the heathen Danes in defence of their country and religion:–

"All the freehold lands of England, except some of those belonging to the Church, were subject to three great public burdens: military service in the kings expeditions, or at least in defensive war; the repair of bridges, and that of royal fortresses. These obligations, and especially the first, have been sometimes thought to denote a feudal tenure. There is, however, a confusion into which we may fall by not sufficiently. discriminating the rights of a king as chief lord of his vassals, and as sovereign of his subjects. In every country, the supreme power is entitled to use the arm of each citizen in the public defence. The usage of all Nations agrees with common reason in establishing this great principle. There is nothing therefore peculiarly feudal in this military service of landholders; it was due from the allodial proprietors upon the continent, it was derived from their German ancestors, it had been fixed, probably, by the legislatures of the Heptarchy upon the first settlement in Britain."

We can easily imagine the Anglo-Saxon kings calling upon the bishops for assistance against the Danes.

The Conquest was followed by the imposition of the feudal system, binding the church to perform military service to the crown. This, at first regarded as a hardship, agreed well with the warlike spirit of the times, and although the bishops appointed their feudal advocates to fight their battles, protect their interests, and lead their vassals to the field, yet they sometimes took the field in person, and rode amid the lances of the men-at-arms. The military advocates held their lands of the church, and, in court and field, their service was honourable. Indeed the title of advocates of the church was bestowed upon Pepin and Charlemagne.

Thus the regulations of the feudal period encouraged the military disposition of the prelates, who, when the invaders burst in, readily raised the cry to arms. It will be remembered that when Hotspur and Douglas carried on their great trial at arms on Otterburne field, by the cloud-drifted light of the moon, the Bishop of Durham was marching with 10,000 men to ensure the defeat of the invaders. However, he arrived too late; the battle was over, Douglas slain, and the two Percies prisoners, and the Scots strongly posted to resist attack. A second battle must have been sanguinary, and the result doubtful, therefore the bishop decided not to take upon himself the responsibility of fighting, but withdrew his warriors, leaving the Scots to return unmolested to their own country.

Chief among the amateur soldiers of the church in King Edward the Firsts days, was the proud and magnificent Bishop of Durham, Anthony de Beck, Patriarch of Jerusalem, and Lord of the Isle of Man. At Falkirk he drew an unrighteous sword against Wallace and the Scottish patriots. Previous to the battle he celebrated a soldiers mass on the field, clothed in knightly mail as he was, the long kite-shaped shield slung over his shoulder, the sword girt at his thigh. The ceremony over, he was ready to charge Wallaces schiltrons and archers, but the first column preceded him, led by the Earl Marshal, and Lincoln, and Hereford. He saw man and horse impaled on the huge Scottish spears, and the charging files rolled back in blood, while the Scottish arrows drifted into their ranks. He appreciated the valour of the enemy, and proposed to await the arrival of the numerous archers, who would speedily, and with little loss to themselves, shoot down the Scottish schiltrons. The men-at-arms were, however, eager to close, and Rudulf Basset scornfully advised the Lord Bishop to stick to his mass, while he led the charge. Thus rebuked, the bishop gave the word, leading, sword-in-hand, and furiously assailed the Scottish left, to be hurled back, again and again. The treacherous retreat of the Scottish cavalry left the schiltrons exposed to certain destruction, and the English archers shot them down without mercy.

When Edward III. lay before Calais, he paid Thomas Hatfield, Bishop of Durham, 6s. 8d. per day, and his following in proportion, viz.:–three bannerets at 4s., 48 knights at 2s., 164 esquires at I2d., 81 archers on horseback at 6d. each per day.

Perhaps the most notable of the fighting bishops was Henry Spencer, of Norwich. When the whole of England lay in panic terror at the mercy of the revolted villeins, when drawbridges were raised, gates closed, and knights and nobles hid themselves behind stone walls, Henry Spencer bade trumpets sound, and sallied forth with his men-at-arms, attacking the marching peasants wherever he met them. Emboldened by his example, a few gentlemen associated themselves with him, and he extended his operations to Cambridge and Huntingdon, which were soon pacified. When John Littester, the dyer, leader of the Norfolk villeins, despatched deputies to the king, the alert bishop intercepted them, and incontinently struck off their heads. A body of the villeins had entrenched themselves at North Walsham. Spencer marched against and stormed their position, being the first to enter, sword-in-hand. A furious and protracted conflict followed, ending in the defeat of the peasants, who were pursued and cut to pieces with unsparing severity. Those spared of the sword and lance Spencer strung up to the nearest tree, first receiving their hurried confession, then granting them absolution. He dispersed the revolted peasantry of Suffolk, and set a marked example to the nobility.

During these events, that man of many enemies, John of Gaunt, had retired into Scotland. So obnoxious was he to the peasantry, that when his wife, Constance of Castille, sought refuge in his Castle of Pontefract, the cowardly retainers refused to admit her, and she had to proceed through a wild country, by torchlight, for night had closed in, to her lords Castle of Knares-borough, where she found a safe haven until Lancasters return.

The ambitious prelate soon found a wider field for his arms.

When, in consequence of a division among the cardinals, two rival popes were elected, Urban VI. and Clement VII., Europe divided on the question, and France and England were naturally in opposition, the former power giving its adhesion to Clement, the latter to Urban, for England feebly strove to retain some portion of the conquests of Edward III. and the Black Prince. Clement, defeated, found refuge at Avignon, and, obedient to his protector, preached a crusade against Richard II. and the English. Urban excommunicated Clement as an anti-pope, and commissioned Bishop Spencer to conduct a crusade against him. The bishop found numerous enthusiastic supporters, and parliament met to consider whether they should ally themselves with the Flemings, or co-operate with Lancaster, from Spain, against the national enemy. The former scheme was adopted, but the French overran Flanders, and beleagured Ghent, the only town that held out against them. Immediate and energetic action was demanded, and the council resolved to support the bishop, who proposed to drive the French out of Flanders, and then carry the war into their own country. For this purpose certain subsidies were be paid to him.

The bishop, however, altered his mind, and proposed, in return for the fifteenth granted by the laity, to serve one year with 2,500 men-at-arms and 2,500 mounted archers. His offer being accepted, William de Beaucham was appointed his lieutenant, and in the month of May, 1383, he carried a body of troops, and numerous volunteers, to Calais, where he awaited the arrival of his lieutenant with the remainder of the forces. These were delayed, it was alleged by the design of John of Gaunt, and the bishop had no alternative but to employ his headstrong and impatient crusaders. Gravelines was assaulted, and carried.

Dunkirk immediately surrendered, but the Count of Flanders, engaged in the interests of France, marched against the crusaders. Sir Hugh de Calverley had reinforced the bishop, and a battle ensued, resulting in the defeat of the enemy, and the surrender of Cassel, Dixmuyde, Bourburg, Newport, and Popperen.

The King of France hastily took the field with 100,000 men, for the position appeared alarming. Norwich had also received succours, forwarded by that gallant merchant, Sir John Philpot, but the new crusaders were rogues and miscreants of the darkest stain, and were influenced by the prospect of unbounded licence and plunder. In his vexation, Spencer requested Philpot to suspend his supply of naked ruffians, but he had to put a bold face on, and match his 90,000 soldiers, crusaders, and thieves, against the army of France. There was, however, a difference of opinion, amounting to a mutiny in the army, and the mortified bishop found himself constrained to besiege Ypres. Several furious assaults were delivered, but the steady courage of the veteran garrison, posted behind strong defences, foiled the fury of the ill-conducted attacks, and the depression of defeat rested upon the army, which avenged itself by casting off all restraint, and spreading over the country for the purpose of plunder, while the pilgrims deserted in large numbers. The French army approached, and the bishop beat a hasty retreat to Dunkirk, leaving his materials of war behind. Bourburg was occupied by Sir Hugh de Calverley and Sir Thomas Trivet, and the King of France closed them in, threatening to put every man to the sword if the place was not immediately surrendered. The threat was vain, and twice the French fell on, to be bloodily repulsed, when King-Charles tendered the garrison quarter, and they marched out and proceeded to Calais. From Bourburg the King carried his army to Gravelines, where he found every prospect of a tough struggle, and wisely concluded to treat rather than fight. The bishop took time to consider the terms proposed, and sent messages to King Richard for succours; but before troops could be collected and embarked, the truce expired, and, agreeable to his undertaking, the bishop dismantled Gravelines, marched the remains of his forces to Calais, and embarked for England.

In Parliament he met with a warm reception for having failed to carry out his engagements, and although his defence entitled him to an honourable acquittal, he was found in default for not having served out his full time, and for the insubordination of his troops. He was mulcted in a severe pecuniary penalty, and the temporalities of his Bishopric were seized. Several of the knights, whose insubordination had tended to produce the miscarriage of the expedition, as Thomas Trivet, Henry Ferners, William Ellingham, and William Harrendon, were fined and imprisoned.

So ended the bishops campaign, in which, however, he manifested the spirit and capacity of a good captain, but success was, with such a soldiery and so powerful an enemy, absolutely impossible.

Pope Martin V. was one of the most determined opponents of the Hussites, and spared no pains in inciting Europe to move in a crusade against those stubborn heretics, whose extermination was most ardently desired.

A. d. 1426, a crusading army was utterly defeated, with a loss of not less than 15,000 men, before the walls of Aussig. The crusaders mustered not less than 70,000 trained soldiers, supported by 180 pieces of artillery, with 3,000 wagons for transport of stores. Quarter was neither given nor accepted, and the defeated and demoralised army was closely pursued. This memorable battle was fought on the forenoon of Sunday, the 16th of June.

"Then fourteen counts and lords of might
Did from their coursers all alight,
Their sword-points deep in earth did place
And to the Czechians sued for grace.
For prayers and cries they cared not aught,
Silver and gold they set at naught,
Een as themselves had made reply,
So every man they did to die."

It was the inhumanity, or bigotry, of the Germans that settled the question of quarter, raised by the Hussites before the battle, and afterwards maintained with unsparing severity.

The Germans having failed, the Pope turned to the English, then winning bloody laurels in France. Henry de Beaufort, Bishop of Winchester, John of Gaunts son, and Henry IV. s brother, was selected for the enterprise. On receiving the Popes bull, he prepared to raise soldiers and money for the crusade. The preaching of the crusade in England met with little or no response. Ready as the islanders were to exchange the rude courtesies of warfare with their Scottish neighbours, to cross the Channel to destroy the armies and ravage the vineyards and cornfields of France, and, earlier, to take the crusaders cross and embark for Palestine, it may be questioned if they had ever a genuine disposition for fighting the battles of the popes. Indeed the friction was rough and frequent between Rome and Britain.

In the city of Mechlin, Beaufort published the papal bull. It was instantly and enthusiastically responded to. A somewhat mixed army was assembled. The figures of the historians, 90,00x3 foot and 90,000 horse, are not easily acceptable, but doubtless the army was a considerable one.

Numerous nobles and knights, including three electors of the empire, marched with and assisted Beaufort, and strengthened the army with their retainers. Perhaps the army lacked cohesion; no doubt its bravest soldiers admitted the terrible might and energy of the foe. Probably those who were not accustomed to arms–townsfolk, artisans, shepherds, and peasants–would be easily influenced by doubt and fear when they found themselves opposed to an enemy whose reputation for valour and severity was so terrible.

Winchester had been created a cardinal, and the Popes legate-a-latere, but he was fated to attain no honour by arms.

Again invaded by a cruel and presumptuous enemy, both Catholics and Hussites united to defend Bohemia.

In the June of 1427, the crusaders crossed the borders, and encamped before Meiss. Although greatly inferior in numbers, the Bohemians advanced and offered battle. The martial appearance of these iron veterans, the knowledge of their dreadful reputation, curiously effected the crusaders. Instead of pushing on to cross the river and open the attack, they stood at gaze. Awed and daunted by the ominous spectacle before them, their ranks shook with a sudden panic, weapons clashed wildly, standards went down. Horse and foot were inextricably mixed as the first of the panic-stricken wretches broke and fled. A dreadful scene followed. Almost in a moment the huge army was transformed into a confused rout of fugitives. As quickly were the waters of the Meiss darkened by the iron ranks of the Hussites as they pressed forward, to fall upon the panic-stricken crusaders with axe and iron-flail, sword and spear, while bullets and arrows were poured incessantly into the flying masses, and the fugitives fell as thick and fast as sere leaves in an autumnal gale.

The crusading army had committed many outrages during the course of its triumphant march, and as the guilty and licentious wretches, losing all order and cohesion, rushed madly before the flashing steel of the pursuers, the peasantry rose against them on every side, pitiless avengers, whose wrath could be alone satiated by blood. The whole of Bohemia was enriched by the enormous spoil of the vanquished.

The Pope, in condoling with Beaufort, spoke hopefully of the success of a new crusade, but the Englishman was satisfied with the extent, if not the character, of his experience.

Richard Scrope had a brief and most unfortunate experience of military operations. His appearance in arms was purely the result of the complications that followed the deposition of Richard II. and the enthronement of Bolingbroke. Lord Scrope, High Chancellor of England, had devotedly served Edward III. and his grandson, Richard of Bordeaux, and after that dark tragedy at Pontefract, that secured, for the time being, the throne of Lancaster, he endowed a chantry in his castle of Bolton, where daily service was performed for the repose of the dead kings soul. The old man was spared, but the kings hand fell heavily upon his sons. First to fall was the Earl of Wiltshire, who was captured in Bristol Castle, and dragged to the block with indecent haste, and on no sufficient cause, by Bolingbrokes command. This alone might have predisposed the Archbishop to ally himself with the Kings enemies, when many of the nobles repented that they had set up the son of John of Gaunt in the place of the son of the heroic Black Prince. The avenging of his brothers blood could scarcely fail to influence the Archbishop, but no doubt he was wrought upon by the Kings enemies, and felt called upon, if not to avenge the slaying of the King, at least to endeavour to correct his government, and arrest the shedding of blood which so deeply stained the early years of Henrys reign.

The princely power of the Archbishops in Northumbria, and the personal esteem in which Scrope was held, made his appearance in arms peculiarly dangerous to the King. Lord Mowbray associated himself with Scrope, and no sooner was the standard of revolt uplifted than the hardy Yorkshiremen flocked to support their Archbishop. Scrope published a terrible and undeniable indictment against the blood-stained Henry. He was accused of treason, usurpation, regicide, the withholding of the crown from the Earl of March, the lineal heir, with other charges not to be refuted.

Ralph, Earl of Westmoreland, and Prince John, were despatched against Scrope and Mowbray, but they found the northern army so formidable that they dared not strike. On approaching the Archbishop they found him ready to enter into negotiations for the correcting of the Kings government, and the Earl of Westmoreland, with a treachery that was. infamous at a time when treachery and perjury were common, pretended to grant all Scropes demands, and, as a ratification of the terms of pacification, proposed the disbanding of the two armies. This was unsuspiciously acceded to, and the northern army was immediately disbanded, although the royal army maintained its formation. Danger of rescue past, the Earl of Westmoreland, with infamous treachery, arrested Scrope, Mowbray, and several of their captains. " The King was then at Pontefract, and when the Archbishop and the other captives were brought thither to him, they were ordered to be carried from thence to York, where they were condemned to death by the judges, Fulford and Gascoign. Judgment was no sooner passed, but the Archbishop was set upon a lean deformed horse, with his face backward; and that Bishop, whose grave age commanded every mans respect, having been always accompanied with holiness of life, incomparable learning, and a lovely person, was now loaded with all sorts of disgrace and reproaches, and so conducted to the place of execution, where his head was cut off, June 8th, 1405, by an unskilful executioner, who scarcely effected it at five strokes. He was buried on the eastern part of the new works, where certain miracles were said to have been done by the merits of this martyr, and the King to be smitten with an incurable leprosy. It is certain he was the first archbishop that was condemned to death by a legal trial. The Pope excommunicated the authors of this archbishops death, but was easily intreated to absolve them a little time after." To augment the bitterness of death, Scrope was removed to his palace of Bishopthorpe for execution, and his head was piked and exposed on the walls of York.

Mowbray, Sir Robert Plumpton, Sir John Lamplugh, and other unfortunates, also suffered decollation.

During the great rebellion that cost Charles Stuart his crown and head, another Archbishop of York took up arms, to figure obscurely during a struggle in which he certainly was not called upon to assume the soldiers painful and difficult part. A changeful and troublous history is that of John Williams. In 1621 he was elevated to the Bishopric of Lincoln, and Lord Keeper of the Great Seal, but his fortunes waned as Laud rose to power; he lost the Seals, and at the coronation of Charles I. it was his duty, as Dean of Westminster, to read divine service, but Laud took his place. He was further affronted by being forbidden to sit in the House, and Laud brought him into the Star Chamber for having written the " Holy Table." He was suspended, fined. 10,000, and imprisoned in the Tower during the Kings pleasure. He obtained his release November 16th, 1640.

Not unnaturally his suffering made him an object of interest to the Puritan party, but he was loyal to Charles, and by preaching before him in condemnation of the discipline of Geneva he won the royal favour, and he was raised to the Archbishopric of York. The evil times had closed in, and for leading the bishops in their protest against the House of Lords, he was committed to the Tower, where he remained some time. Then came the war.

When Captain Hotham and Sir Thomas Fairfax were earning their spurs by the most daring exploits against the Royalists of Yorkshire, Hotham received some cause for offence from the Archbishop, and irefully vowed to cut off his head.

A friendly warning of the threat reached the Archbishop late on the 3rd of October, and, appreciating the spirit of the young dare-devil, the prelate left Cawood Castle in hot haste. Not long after, Hotham and his fiery riders spurred up in hot haste, and finding their intended victim had escaped, they solaced themselves by sacking the castle.

Joining the king at Oxford, Williams received the royal commission and instructions, and proceeded to fortify his castle at Aberconway, but, apparently from some unworthy suspicion of his loyalty, the king appointed another commandant to the castle, and Williams, in deep disgust, retired to his house at Penryn, placed it in a state of defence, and gave in his adhesion to parliament.

Assisted by Colonel Mitton, he besieged Aberga-venny, in South Wales, and reduced the stronghold to the obedience of parliament. He expired at Lady Mostyns house at Gloded, on the 25th of March, 1650, being the 68th anniversary of his birth.

Thus an old Yorkshire history: " While he was in his greatness, he was characterized a person of a generous mind, a lover and encourager of learning and learned men (being himself very learned), hospitable and a great benefactor to the public; but when, through anger and disgust, he sided with the parliament and Puritans, he was styled by the Royalists a perfidious prelate, the shame of the clergy, and the apostate archbishop, which how much he deserved, considering his provocations, let the reader judge. He hath many things in print, etc." Lord Campbell adds this tribute to the memory of this unfortunate prelate, for truly unfortunate he must be esteemed, "He will always be memorable in English history, as the last of a long line of eminent ecclesiastics, who, with rare intervals, held for many centuries the highest judicial office in the kingdom, and exercised a powerful influence over the destinies of the nation."

Such are a few of the romantic and interesting facts relating to the military experience of English bishops, which are scattered through the pages of our national history. In some cases we cannot blame, in others we must actually applaud, our fighting bishops for patriotism, courage, and conduct of no common order; and where we may be disposed to censure, we may justly pause, and weigh the character of the times, the usages of the church, and admit that in their day and generation, they were not acting so opposite to their character and profession as we may be disposed to regard them, if we do so from the higher spiritual conditions of our own more favoured and settled times.

Gbe Cloister anand its Storp.

By S. W. Kershaw, F. s. a.

"The treasures of antiquity laid up
In old historic rolls I opened."

–beaumont.

FAIR and famed are the monastic ruins of our land, from Fountains and Rievaulx among the Yorkshire dales, to Tintern on the silvery Wye, and Netley near the placid Solent, one and all alike tell a tale of their past annals, making up, verily, a treasured page of " Bygone England."

With these buildings are closely connected one of their great agencies, when, as dispensers of learning, in the early ages, darkness and ignorance was all around. Just as the legendary dictum arose, that the exquisite lantern of Ely Cathedral became a guiding light to the traveller, in the fens and morasses of Eastern England, so these religious homes were the beacon spots of learning.

In that remote period of way-faring, it was the custom for some churches to have a fire lighted in an iron framework on the top of an angle turret, to direct the steps of the stranger, especially through those vast woods which covered our land, and of which a famous example existed in the forest of Galtres, in Yorkshire.

The visitor to Gloucester Cathedral will have noticed its exquisite cloisters, and have seen the screens or " carols " where the monkish scribe sat diligently to copy his chronicle, or the artist to illuminate its page.

The examples at Gloucester are almost unique as an illustration, so to speak, of the workshops of the mediaeval copyist; but a "scriptorium," or room, was arranged in most monastic houses, as the more general place of labour.

As the chief homes and nurseries of religion, these houses attracted their different leaders and schools of learning. With Bede in Northumbria, and Augustine in Kent, two great missionary scholars, the memories of ancient lore seem to be recalled. In quick succession arose the vast abbeys of our land, at St. Albans, Glastonbury, York, Canterbury, Lindisfarne, and Hexham, spreading their influence far and wide, with a host of lesser foundations. Their erection, often due to the zeal of some noted ecclesiastic or pious layman, is closely connected with our church history and customs, revealing many a vivid picture of olden days. Their abbots and priors can show many illustrious names, and Matthew Paris, Aldhelm, Bishop of Sherborne, St. Cuth-bert, and William of Malmesbury, are but a tithe of the roll-call of writers and chroniclers.

It is, however, the work which remains to this day as the evidence and link of an almost forgotten agency, through the preservation of our early documents, that the moving history of those times is recalled. The " scriptorium " under the abbots direction, with specially trained scribes, was the great literary workroom, rules and admonitions were hung on its walls, expressive of the care to be taken in copying, the work was portioned out, and no monk could exchange his allotted task for another.

There were those specially selected, to insert the rubricated letters and designs of the border page, while others prepared the vellum, or attended to the binding. In the larger monasteries, especially of the Cistercians, there were smaller " scriptoria" for the more learned of the community, distinguished also by their skill and attainments.

The transcription of Missal or Service books was often made, not only for the great houses, but for the smaller ones, unable to maintain so large a staff, and then both " scriptorium " and cloister became a ceaseless centre of labour. Books were often lent from one monastery to another to be copied, and besides the actual staff, hired writers were also employed, thus rapidly developing the learning of those early times. Special grants of money were made to support this constant occupation–tithes and other aids procured the vellum, the ink, and the colours for the artist; thus, by degrees, came into existence those grand volumes which, despite time and decay, have survived to our day. The abbey chronicle and the abbots letters became one great monastic diary, each containing a record of events and customs which shadowed forth many a noted incident or rare tradition.

In the Christ Church letters, at Canterbury, we hear of Prior Chillendens love of building, and mention of the grey old walls of that city, portions of which are now standing, is found in this correspondence.

Truly can it be said, that the abbey and its literature grew together, that the annals of the one were the foundation stones of the other. The " Chronicle," perhaps the most typical form of monastic work, gave expression to endless literary fragments, some, undoubted forgeries, as one scribe often copied the errors of a preceding writer. The lives of saints, and their legends, were lightly interwoven in this day-book of the religious house, and the famous miracles of Thomas a Becket, repeated in all their varying allurements, formed the staple theme for many a credulous monk.

On the other hand, the " Chronicle" recorded important events, especially the building of a noted minster, oratory, or shrine. Ingulphus treated of Croyland; William of Malmesbury, of Glastonbury; Gervase, the burning of Canterbury, and many like instances. In these volumes we often find allusions to the means used to raise money for building, and the curious customs arising out of this effort. When a cathedral wanted repair, the bishop selected from among his clergy a few preachers, and along with them a saints shrine, in which relics were enclosed and carried by young clerks in procession. On reaching a town, these relics were taken to the church and left on one of the altars, and those who could afford, threw their offerings on the same.

Processions to some noted spot formed another source of revenue, and the picturesque though fanciful custom of strewing the churchyard cross with boughs on Palm Sunday, may have been another of the quaint usages to attract the devotee to make his offerings.

Fairs, too, were held, sometimes in the very cathedral precincts, and mystery and miracle plays also combined to increase the funds required for a grand fabric, or village church. A leading feature in the archivists work were the bishops registers, to be found in every diocese, and varying greatly in their interest and contents. Those of Canterbury and York form a unique collection of church history, while others are models of exactness or statesmanlike precision.

As we turn over their pages, we recall the names of William of Wykeham (Bishop of Winchester), Bishop Alcock (Ely), Chichele, the munificent founder of All Souls, Oxford, while among lesser dignitaries may be classed Abbot Islip, of Westminster, and John of Whethampstead, for St. Albans, whose registers and minute books betoken their care and knowledge, as " Super visors " of the noble buildings under their charge. Perhaps the register of St. Osmund, Bishop of Salisbury (1078-1107), may fairly be taken to represent the idea of what is usually found to illustrate the growth, maintenance, and customs connected with those stately fabrics and minsters of our land. As St. Osmund was one of the prelate-architects, so to speak, and having much to do with the building of that cathedral, there are, naturally, endless allusions to antiquarian lore, indeed, his register can well be likened to a storehouse of local customs, and ecclesiological learning.

On one page is an account of the maintenance of Savernake forest, over which the Dean and chapter of Sarum had certain rights. On another, we find a description of the stones and ornaments for the church, while elsewhere are the charters for the bestowal of land, towards the endowment of canonries and other preferments, and to these last were attached seals of deep historical value.

This register may be taken then as the keystone to the annals of Sarum diocese, and what the keen inquirer finds in this as a typical book, may equally be said of several other episcopal archives. In their silent, though not less expressive, language, they have handed down those incidents on which hang the story of many an effort to build a costly shrine, a sculptured porch, or greater still, the minsters and abbeys which have made England of the past so rich an inheritance for us of to-day.

The fullest scope for the mediaeval artist was found in the pictured chronicle, or the illuminated missal, that task on which painter and scribe devoted their best talents, and with this embellishment is interwoven many an old usage or fanciful legend.

The monastery garden supplied endless designs for the exquisite plant-forms and scrolls which mingled so gracefully with the written text or the printed page. In the gifted words of the late Lady Eastlake, who said, "Here on these solid and well-nigh indestructible parchment folios, where text and picture alternately take up the sacred tale–the text itself a picture, the picture a homily–the skill of the artist has exhausted itself in setting forth the great scheme of salvation."

Flowers also supplied an un-ending theme for symbolism which always allied itself to sacred and legendary art, and tradition asserts that the monks reared an appropriate flower for each holy-day, and that certain flowers were dedicated to saints. The ivy a type of immortality, the oak of virtue and majesty, the lily, and the rose, all had their significance on the vellum book.

" History of Our Lord," by the late Mrs. Jameson, continued by Lady Eastlake.

Mingled with the border designs were satirical allusions in the form of grotesques and other drolleries, evidently aimed at the jealousies of the secular and regular clergy, one against the other, or both against the mendicant friars. What was found on the illuminated page, was echoed in the architectural carvings of the time, and the fantastic wood work in some of our cathedrals and many churches, especially in the stalls of Christ Church, Hants, repeat the teachings of the caustic monk in his cloistered seclusion.

It was reserved for the architect-artist to perpetuate in stone the beauties of the floral world, and nothing speaks a stronger though mute language than the foliage sculptured on the arches, doorways, and nooks of our minsters, churches, and abbey ruins.

"Ivy, and vine, and many a sculptured rose,
The tenderest image of mortality,
"Binding the slender columns, whose light shafts
Cluster like stems in corn-sheaves."

Not only was symbolism embodied in these carvings, but as an exercise and offering of devotion to the Unseen, the best efforts were lavished on it by the skilled master-workmen of the time.

Thus the scribe, the illuminator, the architect were all striving in a kind of companion rivalry, each illustrating by his efforts some phase of artistic labour, or reviving a long-forgotten custom.

However much we may dissociate legend with truth, we cannot always ignore it, mingled though it may be with monkish ignorance and superstition.

The tale of many a noble structure has been veiled under the guise of the chronicle or the monastic ledger book, and the foundation of Waltham Abbey is said to have originated from a 12th century MS., entitled, "De inventione Sancte Crucis." Around the grand church of Minister in Thanet, gathers a pretty story, in that Dompneva, wife of Penda, King of Mercia, asked Ethelbert to grant her land in Thanet, on which she might build a monastery. In answer to how much she required, "Only as much as my deer can run over at one course." The King gave her the wide tract of land run over by the deer, and she founded the cloister on the spot where now stands Minister church. Local names have sometimes been associated with the story of the cloister. The Bell-rock with its lighthouse was so called from the bell which the monks tolled, to warn the mariner of his danger.

The smallest item on the parchment page can have an extended meaning; the sign of the cross was found in many old deeds, which often contained an invocation to the Trinity, and the famous story of St. Helena, and the finding of the cross, has its incidents oft repeated in the MS., the printed book, the panel or fresco painting, as well as in the marvellous pieces of the sacred wood, so greatly venerated by the faithful! Of St. Dunstan, Archbishop of Canterbury, there is a drawing, said to be by his own hand, in the illumination of a manuscript in the Bodleian Library, and of dedication of churches to saints, the name is legion. St. Barnabas Day is specially linked with English life and manners, it was the longest day according to the old style, and the old rhyme,

"Barnaby bright, Barnaby light,
The longest day and the shortest night."

Every form of chronicled lore, be it register, fabric roll, charter, or brief, teems with some peculiar custom which is a moving history, an heirloom from the old world, helping to connect the past and the present.

Architectural items enter largely into the varied forms of church documents; the Indulgence often gave full particulars as to the repairs. of a building, a fact most valuable for supplying the date at which any portion was built or renewed. Cathedral archives of whatever class, are sure to abound in allusions to the fabric or its annals, sometimes going so far as to sketch some portion in the marginal pages, of which an example is found in a drawing of old St. Pauls in the 14th century, occurring in a MS. called the " Flores historiarum." The statutes of our minsters are rich in ecclesiastical lore, the mediaeval fraternities or guilds are often mentioned in them, and in the statutes of St. Pauls a most curious custom is mentioned of waits parading the streets of London, to give notice of the feast of the Transfiguration, and carrying with them a picture or banners of that event.

The antiquarian enthusiast on these subjects cannot do better than consult the work on " English Guilds" published by the Early English Text Society, and that of the " Statutes of St. Pauls," by Dr. Sparrow Simpson, 1873.

Fabric rolls and inventories are an endless source of detailed information, in both of these, most minute descriptions are given; the painting and drawing of images, the materials, even to the pencils and brushes, being mentioned. Perhaps the most elaborate is that of the expense rolls for St. Stephens chapel, in the old palace of Westminster, a bill of charges that helps to identify the kind of work done at that time, and the general artistic treatment in the reign of Edward III.

The following entries may be given as a typical illustration:–

William de Padryngton, mason, for making twenty angels to stand in the tabernacles, by task work at 6/8 per each image. 6 13s. 4d.

For seven hundred leaves of gold, bought for the painting of the tabernacles in the Chapel 1 8s. od.

The following item shows that there were artists who designed the work afterwards carried out by inferior craftsmen.

Hugh de St. Albans and John de Cotton, painters, working on the drawings of several images. o 9s. od.

An examination of this expense roll, of which this is not a tithe of the entries, printed in Smiths history of Westminister, will well repay attention.

With those graceful chantries, which adorn most of our minsters, are closely connected the service books of the middle ages, for it was usual to insert in the blank spaces of the collects the names of the founders of the chantry chapels.

Indeed, the subtle way in which our old documents, of whatever class, interweave themselves with the annals of our mediaeval buildings, whether as regards the general plan, the design of some sculptured porch, the pictured images on walls, or the many-coloured votive chapel, each and all illustrating a quaint legend or significant custom, is too numerous to indicate.

"Nor was all this labour spent in vain; their homes for centuries were in the silence of the sanctuary; their authors have mingled with the dust of the convent cemetery; over them have passed the rise and fall of the kingdoms of this world; but through them history has been transmitted with a continuity and fulness not to be found in any other form of art, or, it may be said in any form of literature."

"Mid all the light a happier age has brought,
We work not yet as our forefathers wrought."

"History of Our Lord," by the late Mrs. Jameson, 1864.

Sbortband in burcb.

By William E. A. Axon, F. r. s. l.

WHEN Job Everardt published in the year 1658, his " Epitome of Stenographic," he had certainly no intention of minimising the value of his art, but, on the contrary, was quite ready to magnify the office of the shorthand writer. The engraved title-page is ornamented by eleven emblematical pictures, and stenography is declared to be " Swifter than the swift of foot" (Amosii. 15); " Swifter than a post" (Job ix. 25); " Swifter than a weavers shuttle " (Job vii. 20); "Swifter than waters" (Job xxiv. 18); "Swifter than clouds" (Isaiah xix. 1); "Swifter than ships " (Job ix. 26); " Swifter than horses " (Jer. iv. 13); " Swifter than dromedaries" (Jer. ii. 23); " Swifter than roes" (1 Chron. xii. 8); "Swifter than leopards " (Heb. i. 8); " Swifter than eagles " (2 Sam. i. 23). It may be remarked in passing that the worthy Everardt consistently spells than then in the text to each of these emblems. We have left to the last the picture which holds the place of honour. Here we see a worthy divine, robed in a black gown, set off with white collars and cuffs, and with his head covered by a furred skull cap. He stands in a low pulpit, his hands rest on the comfortable cushion, which is unencumbered either by book or MS. Opposite to him, and occupying the whole of a comfortable form or very wide chair, is a stenographer. He wears his hat, as was often customary in church during the seventeenth century; he has impressive white hands; he has not taken off his cloak, but on a fold of it allows a book to rest, in which, with an impossible pen, he is taking down the sermon, and stares with fixed gaze as the divine asserts " My tongue is as the pen of a swift writer," and seems almost inclined to dispute the assertion that any tongue could keep pace with his nimble stylus.

It must be confessed that the early stenographers–to confine our attention to them–were not at all in the habit of under-valuing their art. Here is what this same Everardt, " dropping into poetry" like Silas Wegg, has to say in a triple acrostic:–

Secret, short, swift this Writer is, the Suns course seemes but slow to his The Teachers nimble tongue comes short this Writer waits his next report Eagles are swift, his pen doth flee his quill an Eagles seems to bb Noe clouds can flee, Nor waters run swifter then his quick strokes have don One posting Swiflly TO and fro his Oft-turnd quill doth even SO Galley or ship with Sailes and Flagg the Weavers shuttle, Leopard, Stagg Roe, Dromedary, Horse or Har: or the swift swiming Dolphin rar And the quick Scribes, As Shemaja Baruch, Ezra, ELISHAMA Paint forth, as Patterns in a map this ARTS true Portrature and shap Haste Haste to learn what it doth teach Swiftness and Shortness both to reach Yea both in Stenography LY much more in this EPITOMY

After this ingenious torturing of the Queens English, it is not surprising to find,

"In steed sic of Tenne command"-Lords Pray r, Creed: Heers Three and Thirty Languages to Reade,"

that is to say, the sentence " But the just shall live by his faith," in that number of tongues, first in his stenographic characters, and then transliterated into longhand. His dedication is written in the style of a sermon, and in an introductory verse he does not fail to claim that by his art are

". Sermons writ even from the lip,
And sudden thoughts before they slip."

His good opinion of his own stenography, and powers of versification, sustains him to the end of his book, and he bids us adieu in this wise:–

"Herewith Farewell; If you can tell
What yet more fair, short, swift maybee,
Let the world know it, candedly sic show it
Or if not, Follow this with mee."

William Hopkins "Flying Penman" (1695), has the following commendation signed by one whose surname has since become famous in divinity:–

"Virgil, who largely wrot about the Gnat
That saveing Mans life his own ruine gat,
Might have emploid his pen about this Fly
With greater pleasure and Utility,
A Fly this is, but of more noble kind
Than in the winged crue you ere did find:
A Flying Man; the Flying-Pen-man tis
VVhose wing the fleeing game doth never miss.
The Eagle strikes down and eats up his prey
Destroying all that he doth bear away,
Bui what this Pen-man takes he doth preserve,
And makes it better to all uses serve,
When fleeting words would vanish with their sound
He doth them stay, and them deliver bound,
By Lines of Characters wherein they rest
As in a dwelling that doth please them best.
The Art of Spelling at first was thought
Strange, and they deemd immortal who it taught,
Spelling by Characters excelleth all
That under any other Art doth fall.
Some Charactors creep, some go, these do Fly
Showing their authors great agility,

And this ability he doth impart
By certain rules of a defusive Art."
   Edward Beecher.

   Hopkins gives a long list of theological words, and of abbreviations of such phrases as " the blood of the saints," "the breath of the Almighty," "the candle of the Lord," etc. In reporting the words of preachers, he advises the use of a book, with a margin ruled off, in which to "set down the numbers and names of all the heads contained in the sermon. All these heads," he says, "with parts of the Inlargements used upon them may be taken by such who hardly ever wrote before." This statement must be received cum grano sails. The system best known as that of Jeremiah Rich, who appears to have copied it from his uncle, William Cartwright, was one that seems to have been favoured by the divines of the seventeenth century. It was modified by Dr. Dodd-ridge, and taught in his academy for the training of Nonconformist ministers, and then came into use in most of the older dissenting colleges, so that twenty years ago there were many who had thus been trained and conned the dumpty little bibles and psalm books that were engraved in Richs system. That system has had many names attached to it. Let us take that which bears the impress of " Botleys learned hand." One of his eulogists tells us

   "Sermons this art transfers, its oft known
The countrey reaps whats in the City sowne;
   "The sacred pulpit is not its confine
The general good is this arts main designe."

   Botleys " Maximum in Minimo," which appeared in 1659, is avowedly Jeremiah Richs " Pens dexterity compleated." The theological uses of the system are further asserted by ingenious devices for indicating such phrases as " to be joyned in love to those that are not of the people of God," " to embrace the cross of Christ," etc. This character = Q signifies " to be miserable as the world is miserable," whilst A meant "a saint is a 1000 times better than the world." So in Noah Bridges " Stenographic," issued in the same year, there are phraseograms for "in the name of the Lord," "wherefore said the psalmist," etc.

   The "New Method of Short and Swift Writing," which was given away to purchasers of Dr. Chamberlens " anodyne necklace for childrens teeth," is declared to be "necessary for all Ministers of State, Members of Parliament, Lawyers, Divines, Students, Tradesmen, Shopkeepers, Travellers, and in fine, all sorts of persons from the highest to the lowest quality, degree, rank, station, and condition whatsoever, and write down presently whatever they hear or see done." The theologian here is somewhat lost in an indiscriminate crowd.

   That shorthand was used for the purpose of obtaining copies both of plays and of sermons in the seventeenth century is sufficiently well-known. There is a curious tract, which professes to be a shorthand report of a discourse, by no less a person than our " Cromwell, chief of men," and although it is but a satire, its curious titlepage is nevertheless evidence of the common belief,–founded doubtless on the common practice,–that stenography could secure verbatim reports of the exhortations of preachers, whether clerical or lay. The tract professes to be,–

"A most Learned, Conscientious and Devout Exercise or Sermon of Self-Denyal, (Preached or) Held forth the last Lords-day of April, in the year of Freedom the 1st, 1649. At Sir P. T. s House in Lincolns-Inn-Fields. By Lieutenant General Oliver Cromwell, Immediately before his going for Ireland, as it was then faithfully taken in Characters, By Aaron Gueredo. And now published for the Benefit of the New Polonian Association, and late Famed Ignoramus furies of this city. Humbly Dedicated to the Worthy Protestant-Hop-Merchants, and the rest of the Ignoramus-Brethren. London: Printed in the Year of Freedom 43."

The sermons of Tobias Crisp, which gave rise to a long controversy, were printed from " short writing," in 1642-43, and also those of Stephen Crisp, the Quaker, in 1694.

The quarrel between-the preacher and the reporter was not long in breaking out. Here is the indignant complaint of Dr. Calamy in the preface of one of his discourses.–

"The iniquity of the times hath necessitated the printing of the ensuing Sermon. There is a Fellow, (who he is I know not) who hath for his own private advantage, published it very imperfectly and corruptly. And herein hath not only sinned against the 8th Commandment in taking away another mans goods without his leave, but also against the gth Commandment, in bearing false witness against his neighbour. For he makes me to say not only such things which I never said, but which are very absurd and irrational. As for example: That the Body is the worse part of the Soul. That the party deceased had not only dona sanaia, but selutifera. That I should tell a story of one good Pell, a Minister, born without doubt in Utopia, for of such a man I never either read or heard. To make some satisfaction to the living and the dead, here you have the same sermon in a truer edition with some few additions then omitted for want of time. If this unhappy necessity may contribute anything to thy good, or to the perpetuating of the Memory of the Reverend, Learned, and godly Minister (at whose Funeral it was preached), I shall not much repent for what I have done, though I am assured, that he that brought me into this necessity, hath cause to repent of this, his irregular and unwarrantable practice. (" The Saints Transfiguration," a Sermon preached at the Funeral of Dr. Samuel Bolton, by Edmund Calamy, B. d., October 19, 1654. London, 1655)."

The preacher had of course alluded to Conradus Pellicanus, the German theologian, whose name the stenographer had but partially caught, and set down as " Pell!" Hinc illae lachrymae–of angry indignation.

The stenographers of the last century followed closely in the footsteps of their predecessors. James Westons " Stenography " of which various editions appeared between 1727 and 1740, has an engraving showing a cathedral, in which a be-wigged divine is preaching to a crowd of fashionably dressed ladies and gentlemen, many of whom are busy with pen and notebook. Underneath the picture is the motto,–

"Be perfect in this useful art, and then
No word from pulpit can escape your pen."

This idea was conveyed by Aulay Macaulay, whose " Polygraphy" has for a frontispiece a pretty engraving, in which two gentlemen and a lady are seen taking down the words which, from the preachers gestures, we may suppose to be both impressive and profitable.

In the nineteenth century, as in the seventeenth, the church is much frequented by stenographers, but more it is to be feared for practice in shorthand than for perfection in piety. The first ambition of the boy who is learning short hand is to "report" a sermon by the preacher whose ministry he attends. Mr. Thomas Allen Reed has given an amusing account of his first exploit in this direction, when he was still struggling with the early difficulties of the system he soon after abandoned for phonography. He says, "I did not, however, relinquish my practice, and in a few weeks I resolved on making a grand attempt to take down the Sunday sermon. I rose early jn the morning with the sense of a weighty responsibility resting upon me. I sharpened my pencil with the gravity of a senator, and folded several sheets of paper together, in the profound conviction that I was undertaking a serious, if not a formidable, duty. I did my best to conceal my emotions, but my heart was beating all the way to the church. As to the preliminary service, I understood as little of it as if it had been read in Cherokee. I stood when I ought to have knelt, and knelt when I should have sat or stood, and demeaned myself like a youth whose religious education had been sadly neglected. At length the clergyman entered the pulpit, and I took my sheets of paper from the Bible in which I had concealed them, and my pencil from my pocket. If I did not feel like Bonapartes soldiers, that the eyes of posterity were upon me, I devoutly believed that every eye in the church was directed to my note book. The colour mounted my cheeks (as it very often did at that period of my life,) and my whole frame trembled. I had a strong impulse to abandon my project, but I summoned all my energy to the task, and awaited the commencement of the sermon. The 12th chapter of Isaiah and the 3rd verse, said the minister in solemn tones. This presented no great difficulty. I am sorry to say that, stenographically speaking, I burked Isaiah, and contented myself with the long-hand abbreviation, Is., and as to the text itself, I thought the first three words would suffice. And now for the sermon. The remarkable words, my brethren, of this important prophecy. Laboriously I followed the deliberate utterances of the speaker, but when I reached the prophecy I floundered about in a maze of dire confusion. I thought it began with ph, and I accordingly started as I had been instructed, with the stenographic equivalent, f, but, finding that this would not do, I crossed it out. Then I tried p, r, and getting a good deal confused, plunged madly into the alphabet, the result being a combination of characters altogether beyond description. But where was the preacher? Away in the distance, almost out of sight and hearing. I was fairly beaten, but not quite disheartened. When another sentence was begun I made a fresh start, this time I was pulled up by the word synonymous, I knew there were some ns and ms in it, but not how many. I must have written three or four of each, and while I was jerking out these segments of circles (their forms were the same as in Phonography,) the clergyman was remorselessly pursuing the intricacies of a long sentence, which I was compelled wholly to abandon. I made several other efforts with the like result. At length I secured an entire sentence of about twenty words, and felt very proud of the achievement. Some half-dozen such sentences rewarded my labour during the sermon. How I racked my brain in the afternoon in poring over these fragments! My memory (not then a bad one) was utterly useless. I had not the slightest conception of the drift of the sermon, but I was determined to make some kind of a transcript, and it was made. I presented it to my mother as my first attempt, and I believe she kept it carefully locked up in a drawer among her treasures. It was fortunate for my reputation that it never afterwards saw the light." (Leaves from the Notebook of Thomas Allen Reed, vol. 1, p. 12; vol. 2, p. 24).

The professional reporting of sermons is now an important department of the stenographers work. The late Mr. Spurgeons sermons were thus reported Iby Mr. Reed. Dr. Gumming had his own reporter, as had Beecher, and as Talmage and others have. Dr. Joseph Parkers discourses were "specially reported" by his wife. It is to the phonographic skill of a lady that we owe the preservation of many of the lectures, sermons, and prayers of the late George Dawson. The sermons of the Rev. Thomas T. Lynch were also reported by Mr. Reed. Yet the preacher had a strong dislike to his discourses being reported and printed, " especially without his revision." There, no doubt, is the rub. Dr. Morley Punshon had a strong dislike to be reported, and some letters that passed between him and Mr. Reed are given in the Phonetic Journal, July 3Oth, 1881. His objections were that the reporter was sometimes inaccurate, and that the preacher alone had a right to decide whether he would or would not address the larger congregation to be reached by the press. And he urged very strongly that the arguments used by Macaulay as to the unauthorised publication of his speeches were equally applicable to the case of sermons. It is still a rather doubtful point whether sermons are covered by the law of copyright, and many single sermons and even volumes have been published without the sanction, and sometimes against the wishes, of the preachers. But as it has been held by the law courts that a professors lectures cannot be legally published without his consent, it is possible that some day a preacher may arise who will test the question and ask the judges to say if the pulpit is as much protected as the teachers desk. The late Bishop Eraser is said to have jocularly declared that there was no heresy that had not been attributed to him by the slips of note-takers and condensers.

Shorthand has been extensively used for the MS. of preachers, as by Dr. Chalmers, Job Orton, and a host of other preachers,–so many, indeed, that to deal with stenography in the pulpit would need a larger space than is here available.

Perhaps the most original use of shorthand in church was that due to the conscientiousness and business instincts of the late Rt. Hon. W. H. Smith. Ecclesiastical patronage he felt to be a great responsibility. When there was a minister to be appointed he sought the best information as to those who were recommended to him as suitable. Sometimes he corresponded with friends likely to know; "at other times he used to send his confidential shorthand writer to attend the services of clergymen who might be suitable for the vacancy, and bring him verbatim reports of the sermons, with confidential memoranda of their appearance, views, abilities, and other details. It was only after carefully examining this information that he would proceed to make the appointment."

Those clergymen who owed their promotion to the testimonials thus obtained might say with Job Ortons pious fervour, "Blessed be God for shorthand."

1Reminiscence0 of our Milage Cburcb.

By The Rev. Canon Benham, B. c., F. s. a.

I PROPOSE in the following notes to write my recollections of a village church. They extend over nearly sixty years, and will, no doubt, describe a growth and change which might have been observed in a thousand English churches.

But first, let me say a few words of this church before my recollection of it; not long before, for I am indebted to my mothers reminiscences for the few trifles with which I open. It was a heavy looking edifice, not attractive to the eye as compared with the " storied windows, richly dight," which mark the churches of the beautiful Gothic revival of our own times. This was a plain building, flint, with queer old stone facings, a heavy tower, "churchwarden" windows with diamond panes, with not an atom of beautiful tracery from one end to the other.

And yet that church, if you had been taught how to look for it, contained features of the deepest interest to an antiquary. Within, were heavy Norman pillars between nave and aisles, and a round-headed flattened chancel arch, unmistakably Saxon. For that church was built by S. Wilfred of York in the 8th century, and built so substantially, that there it was in the igth century, sturdy and strong, though successive generations had bepewed it and begalleried it, and put in square ugly windows, and a three-decker, in fact, had used their utmost endeavours to disfigure it. They could not destroy the simple Norman capitals, but they had whitewashed them, and had written up, with the best intentions, texts on the walls, in which my youthful eyes discovered two or three blunders in spelling. It is no wonder that the old Rector, who liked to see everything graceful and artistic, but who had never learned the principles of Architecture scientifically, failed to appreciate S. Wilfreds ancient work, and yearned to see something more graceful in its place. But of that presently. Let me go back for eighty years. The incumbent in those days was an old foxhunter, very fat and of enormous appetite. One day he came in from a long run across country. " Wilthon," said he (he used to lisp) "What ith there for my dinner?" "A goose, sir," said Wilson. "Bring him up, Wilthon, Ill goothe him." And he finished the goose and picked every bone clean. A well-known politician, who died only recently, was born in the village, and the old rector was called on to baptize him. " Name thith child," said he, and the answer was duly given, "James Edwin Thorold." The rector stared, for such exuberance of nomenclature was very uncommon in those days. "What?" he said in amazement. The name was repeated. " Bleth my thoul, what a lot of nameth," said he, " thay it onthe more." The name was said a third time, and the baby was duly christened. A lady who witnessed this, and who still lives, told me of this. She was twelve years old. My grandfather, in those days, was leader of the choir. They sat in a gallery, and had a fiddler and a trombone to accompany them. The trial of Queen Caroline, in 1820, raised the passions of the whole country to fever heat, and the rustics, for the most part, took the queens side. When the news came down, that Government had abandoned the " bill of pains and penalties " for depriving her of the title of queen, there were processions through the street, and every window that did not display a candle, by way of illumination, got a stone through it. On the following Sunday my grandfather gave out the Psalm, which of course was Tate and Bradys, "35th Psalm, nth and three following verses, False witnesses with, forged complaints." It was sung with tremendous energy, and the old rector was furious, not unreasonably, and sent the whole choir to Coventry for some time. He used to put on his surplice in the chancel, before the people, and exchange it in the reading desk for the black gown, and used to preach one sermon on Sundays. He died about 1826, and was succeeded by one who was a brilliant scholar, a canon of a northern Cathedral, and a man who according to his lights was zealous for the decencies of worship. Thus he built a vestry, put the clerk into a black gown, and started a verger with a long coat and red collar, knee breeches, and a long staff of office, who always preceded him to the reading desk. I am now come within the sphere of my own recollections. This old rector lived until 1844, and my early ideas of the proprieties of the church service were all drawn from him. For he had a reason for everything, and expressed it pleasantly, and he was very kind to me personally. Is it any wonder that for many a year I tried all questions of ritual–I am not sure that I have ceased even now–with " What would Doctor B. have thought about this? " He never preached one sermon in the church during his whole incumbency. I understood that it was the danger of a sudden failure of voice, to which he was subject, that prevented-him. Anyhow that was the fact. But he established afternoon sermons, and his curate always preached them. He himself used regularly to say the Prayers, and never since his day have I ever heard anybody read the lessons so well as he did. I never hear the first chapter of the Hebrews without recalling the magnificent roll of his voice, as he brought out of it the points of the opening argument. He was keen upon chanting, and vocal music, and we always sang the Canticles, and the metrical Psalms–as I think very well–and a few Sanctuses. The only case of chanting the Prayer Book Psalms was certainly curious. He had heard in Westminster Abbey, the 137th Psalm, "By the waters of Babylon," sung to a chant which much delighted him, and on the 28th day of the month, when that Psalm occurs, we chanted it to the music referred to. All the other Psalms were read.

We used to be told at school that on Sundays we got a taste of Heaven, for we went to church and sang Gods praises. I do not quarrel with the teaching even now, I think there is something in it. But I used to think, in those tender pinafore years, that in Heaven there would be one improvement, namely, that we should not stand on cold damp stones and feel half perished. There were forms running up the centre of the church, the whole length of it, on the cold bricks, no arrangement at all for kneeling, and on these forms we sat during lessons, prayers, sermon; and many a cold in the head did I catch. The best singers among the boys, of whom I was not one, went into the gallery. The old Rector established a school in the village, and we learned the Tonic Sol-Fa, and the singing was said to be the best for miles round. I think it was in 1842, two years before his death, that the fiddles and clarionettes were disestablished, and the music was entirely vocal.

There was one feature of his incumbency which I must not forget, I mean his church catechising. It had always been a favourite doctrine of his, that catechising in church should be a feature of church work, and every Sunday afternoon in Lent, the boys were marshalled round the reading desk and catechised. Perhaps rather unfortunately, he had a keen sense of fun, and occasionally a bit of humour in his questions, or his comments, set the congregation in a titter. But there was no question that those who listened picked up a great amount of Biblical and ecclesiastical knowledge.

One mistake as I know now, the dear old rector made. He did not know of the archaeological interest of the church, disfigured as it had been by country carpenters and painters and white-washers, and he built a new one, designed by Sir G. Gilbert Scott, then a very young man. And so S. Wilfreds Church was pulled down, and a modern building, handsome enough, has taken its place. But before it was finished the old rector died. So now my recollections pass on to another building and another idea of service.

The new church was certainly more comfortable for the schoolboys, and the singing still continued good. But the new rector made some alterations in matters on which his predecessors had been strong. He was a very pronounced Puritan, and forbade the school children to turn eastward for the Creeds. He forbade such simple anthems as "Lord of all power and might," and Cecils " I will arise." But he had his very good points. He was young and active, and visited his people assiduously, established a monthly Communion, and worked up a regular branch of the Church Missionary Society, which nobody in the village had ever heard of before. I grew up to manhood during his incumbency, and though I regarded his Puritan practices, and listened to his Calvinistic sermons and tirades against Popery with extreme dislike, I see now that he was a man who was most faithful to his convictions, and no man could be more earnest for the spiritual welfare of his people. He was no scholar, I doubt whether he could have read a page of the Greek Testament in his later days. But he was the kind friend of the sick and the aged, and looked after the young people of his flock, and when they went forth into the world gave them loving and sensible counsels. His wife was as sweet and saintly a character as ever I knew, and their large family have all proved the wisdom of their training. One son has earned himself a name as respected as it is widely known.

His successor was a man of like views, better read, and a kindly-hearted man. But he was less in his parish. Though he kept no curate, he was constantly absent as a "missionary deputation," and his congregation, who had never been instructed in church principles, fell away. He died, and his successor, who was only there for a year or two, was, I am told, a failure, greatly owing to weak health; and so we come down to present times. An organ has been given to the church, thanks to a generous layman; the choir march in procession to their places in the chancel, they do a respectable choral service, and of course turn eastward for their Creed. The parson looks thoroughly well after them, and loves them. There are regular week-day services, and a fair attendance on holy days, and the Sunday congregation is steadily increasing. It had gone down terribly.

Such is an impartial review of the church life in an out-of-the-way country village. My own special old Rector (for I owe more to him than I could ever tell), the builder of the church, was one of the original movers in the celebrated movement of!833, was in fact one of the persons present at the meeting at Hadleigh Rectory, under the presidency of Hugh James Rose, which led to the starting of the Tracts for the Times.

His name appears both in Palmers Narrative, and in Newmans Correspondence. He was a great friend of John Keble. But as the Tract Movement declined visibly towards Rome he

regarded it with increasing dislike, and in his last years expressed that dislike with emphasis. I have sometimes wondered what position he would take up if he lived in our own day, and am inclined to think that the present Archbishop of Canterbury would be regarded by him as best expressing his own views. Peace to them every one, everlasting Light and Rest.

LIST OF PUBLICATIONS
WILLIAM ANDREWS and CO., THE HULL PRESS.
SECOND EDITION. Bound in cloth gilt, demy 8vo. 6s.
Studies of Curious Customs, Services, and Records,
By WILLIAM ANDREWS, F. R. H. S.,
Author Of " Historic Romance," " Famous Frosts And
Frost Fairs," " Historic Yorkshire," Etc.
CONTENTS:

Early Religious Plays: being the Story of the English Stage in its Church Cradle Days–The Caistor Gad-Whip Manorial Service–Strange Serpent Stories–Church Ales–Rush Bearing–Fish in Lent–Concerning Doles–Church Scrambling Charities–Briefs–Bells and Beacons for Travellers by Night–Hour Glasses in Churches–Chained Books in Churches–Funeral Effigies–Torchlight Burials–Simple Memorials of the Early. Dead–The Romance of Parish Registers–Dog Whippers and Sluggard Wakers–Odd Items from Old Accounts–A carefully compiled

Lightning Source UK Ltd.
Milton Keynes UK
28 January 2011

166581UK00001B/129/P